# Guest List Planner

Name

Address

Telephone Number

E-mail Address

Gift

| Save The Day Card Sent | Invitation Sent | R.S.V.P Received | Thank You Sent | Number Attending |
| --- | --- | --- | --- | --- |
| | | | | |

Name

Address

Telephone Number

E-mail Address

Gift

| Save The Day Card Sent | Invitation Sent | R.S.V.P Received | Thank You Sent | Number Attending |
| --- | --- | --- | --- | --- |
| | | | | |

Name

Address

Telephone Number

E-mail Address

Gift

| Save The Day Card Sent | Invitation Sent | R.S.V.P Received | Thank You Sent | Number Attending |
| --- | --- | --- | --- | --- |
| | | | | |

Name

Address

Telephone Number

E-mail Address

Gift

| Save The Day Card Sent | Invitation Sent | R.S.V.P Received | Thank You Sent | Number Attending |
| --- | --- | --- | --- | --- |
| | | | | |

Name

Address

Telephone Number

E-mail Address

Gift

| Save The Day Card Sent | Invitation Sent | R.S.V.P Received | Thank You Sent | Number Attending |
| --- | --- | --- | --- | --- |
| | | | | |

# Guest List Planner

Name

Address

Telephone Number

E-mail Address

Gift

| Save The Day Card Sent | Invitation Sent | R.S.V.P Received | Thank You Sent | Number Attending |
| --- | --- | --- | --- | --- |
| | | | | |

Name

Address

Telephone Number

E-mail Address

Gift

| Save The Day Card Sent | Invitation Sent | R.S.V.P Received | Thank You Sent | Number Attending |
| --- | --- | --- | --- | --- |
| | | | | |

Name

Address

Telephone Number

E-mail Address

Gift

| Save The Day Card Sent | Invitation Sent | R.S.V.P Received | Thank You Sent | Number Attending |
| --- | --- | --- | --- | --- |
| | | | | |

Name

Address

Telephone Number

E-mail Address

Gift

| Save The Day Card Sent | Invitation Sent | R.S.V.P Received | Thank You Sent | Number Attending |
| --- | --- | --- | --- | --- |
| | | | | |

Name

Address

Telephone Number

E-mail Address

Gift

| Save The Day Card Sent | Invitation Sent | R.S.V.P Received | Thank You Sent | Number Attending |
| --- | --- | --- | --- | --- |
| | | | | |

# Guest List Planner

Name

Address

Telephone Number

E-mail Address

Gift

| Save The Day Card Sent | Invitation Sent | R.S.V.P Received | Thank You Sent | Number Attending |
|---|---|---|---|---|

Name

Address

Telephone Number

E-mail Address

Gift

| Save The Day Card Sent | Invitation Sent | R.S.V.P Received | Thank You Sent | Number Attending |
|---|---|---|---|---|

Name

Address

Telephone Number

E-mail Address

Gift

| Save The Day Card Sent | Invitation Sent | R.S.V.P Received | Thank You Sent | Number Attending |
|---|---|---|---|---|

Name

Address

Telephone Number

E-mail Address

Gift

| Save The Day Card Sent | Invitation Sent | R.S.V.P Received | Thank You Sent | Number Attending |
|---|---|---|---|---|

Name

Address

Telephone Number

E-mail Address

Gift

| Save The Day Card Sent | Invitation Sent | R.S.V.P Received | Thank You Sent | Number Attending |
|---|---|---|---|---|

# Guest List Planner

Name

Address

Telephone Number

E-mail Address

Gift

| Save The Day Card Sent | Invitation Sent | R.S.V.P Received | Thank You Sent | Number Attending |
| --- | --- | --- | --- | --- |
|  |  |  |  |  |

Name

Address

Telephone Number

E-mail Address

Gift

| Save The Day Card Sent | Invitation Sent | R.S.V.P Received | Thank You Sent | Number Attending |
| --- | --- | --- | --- | --- |
|  |  |  |  |  |

Name

Address

Telephone Number

E-mail Address

Gift

| Save The Day Card Sent | Invitation Sent | R.S.V.P Received | Thank You Sent | Number Attending |
| --- | --- | --- | --- | --- |
|  |  |  |  |  |

Name

Address

Telephone Number

E-mail Address

Gift

| Save The Day Card Sent | Invitation Sent | R.S.V.P Received | Thank You Sent | Number Attending |
| --- | --- | --- | --- | --- |
|  |  |  |  |  |

Name

Address

Telephone Number

E-mail Address

Gift

| Save The Day Card Sent | Invitation Sent | R.S.V.P Received | Thank You Sent | Number Attending |
| --- | --- | --- | --- | --- |
|  |  |  |  |  |

# Guest List Planner

Name

Address

Telephone Number

E-mail Address

Gift

| Save The Day Card Sent | Invitation Sent | R.S.V.P Received | Thank You Sent | Number Attending |
| --- | --- | --- | --- | --- |

Name

Address

Telephone Number

E-mail Address

Gift

| Save The Day Card Sent | Invitation Sent | R.S.V.P Received | Thank You Sent | Number Attending |
| --- | --- | --- | --- | --- |

Name

Address

Telephone Number

E-mail Address

Gift

| Save The Day Card Sent | Invitation Sent | R.S.V.P Received | Thank You Sent | Number Attending |
| --- | --- | --- | --- | --- |

Name

Address

Telephone Number

E-mail Address

Gift

| Save The Day Card Sent | Invitation Sent | R.S.V.P Received | Thank You Sent | Number Attending |
| --- | --- | --- | --- | --- |

Name

Address

Telephone Number

E-mail Address

Gift

| Save The Day Card Sent | Invitation Sent | R.S.V.P Received | Thank You Sent | Number Attending |
| --- | --- | --- | --- | --- |

# Guest List Planner

Name

Address

Telephone Number

E-mail Address

Gift

| Save The Day Card Sent | Invitation Sent | R.S.V.P Received | Thank You Sent | Number Attending |
| --- | --- | --- | --- | --- |

Name

Address

Telephone Number

E-mail Address

Gift

| Save The Day Card Sent | Invitation Sent | R.S.V.P Received | Thank You Sent | Number Attending |
| --- | --- | --- | --- | --- |

Name

Address

Telephone Number

E-mail Address

Gift

| Save The Day Card Sent | Invitation Sent | R.S.V.P Received | Thank You Sent | Number Attending |
| --- | --- | --- | --- | --- |

Name

Address

Telephone Number

E-mail Address

Gift

| Save The Day Card Sent | Invitation Sent | R.S.V.P Received | Thank You Sent | Number Attending |
| --- | --- | --- | --- | --- |

Name

Address

Telephone Number

E-mail Address

Gift

| Save The Day Card Sent | Invitation Sent | R.S.V.P Received | Thank You Sent | Number Attending |
| --- | --- | --- | --- | --- |

# Guest List Planner

Name

Address

Telephone Number

E-mail Address

Gift

| Save The Day Card Sent | Invitation Sent | R.S.V.P Received | Thank You Sent | Number Attending |
| --- | --- | --- | --- | --- |

Name

Address

Telephone Number

E-mail Address

Gift

| Save The Day Card Sent | Invitation Sent | R.S.V.P Received | Thank You Sent | Number Attending |
| --- | --- | --- | --- | --- |

Name

Address

Telephone Number

E-mail Address

Gift

| Save The Day Card Sent | Invitation Sent | R.S.V.P Received | Thank You Sent | Number Attending |
| --- | --- | --- | --- | --- |

Name

Address

Telephone Number

E-mail Address

Gift

| Save The Day Card Sent | Invitation Sent | R.S.V.P Received | Thank You Sent | Number Attending |
| --- | --- | --- | --- | --- |

Name

Address

Telephone Number

E-mail Address

Gift

| Save The Day Card Sent | Invitation Sent | R.S.V.P Received | Thank You Sent | Number Attending |
| --- | --- | --- | --- | --- |

# Guest List Planner

Name

Address

Telephone Number

E-mail Address

Gift

| Save The Day Card Sent | Invitation Sent | R.S.V.P Received | Thank You Sent | Number Attending |
| --- | --- | --- | --- | --- |

Name

Address

Telephone Number

E-mail Address

Gift

| Save The Day Card Sent | Invitation Sent | R.S.V.P Received | Thank You Sent | Number Attending |
| --- | --- | --- | --- | --- |

Name

Address

Telephone Number

E-mail Address

Gift

| Save The Day Card Sent | Invitation Sent | R.S.V.P Received | Thank You Sent | Number Attending |
| --- | --- | --- | --- | --- |

Name

Address

Telephone Number

E-mail Address

Gift

| Save The Day Card Sent | Invitation Sent | R.S.V.P Received | Thank You Sent | Number Attending |
| --- | --- | --- | --- | --- |

Name

Address

Telephone Number

E-mail Address

Gift

| Save The Day Card Sent | Invitation Sent | R.S.V.P Received | Thank You Sent | Number Attending |
| --- | --- | --- | --- | --- |

# Guest List Planner

Name

Address

Telephone Number

E-mail Address

Gift

| Save The Day Card Sent | Invitation Sent | R.S.V.P Received | Thank You Sent | Number Attending |
| --- | --- | --- | --- | --- |

Name

Address

Telephone Number

E-mail Address

Gift

| Save The Day Card Sent | Invitation Sent | R.S.V.P Received | Thank You Sent | Number Attending |
| --- | --- | --- | --- | --- |

Name

Address

Telephone Number

E-mail Address

Gift

| Save The Day Card Sent | Invitation Sent | R.S.V.P Received | Thank You Sent | Number Attending |
| --- | --- | --- | --- | --- |

Name

Address

Telephone Number

E-mail Address

Gift

| Save The Day Card Sent | Invitation Sent | R.S.V.P Received | Thank You Sent | Number Attending |
| --- | --- | --- | --- | --- |

Name

Address

Telephone Number

E-mail Address

Gift

| Save The Day Card Sent | Invitation Sent | R.S.V.P Received | Thank You Sent | Number Attending |
| --- | --- | --- | --- | --- |

# Guest List Planner

Name

Address

Telephone Number

E-mail Address

Gift

| Save The Day Card Sent | Invitation Sent | R.S.V.P Received | Thank You Sent | Number Attending |
|---|---|---|---|---|
| | | | | |

Name

Address

Telephone Number

E-mail Address

Gift

| Save The Day Card Sent | Invitation Sent | R.S.V.P Received | Thank You Sent | Number Attending |
|---|---|---|---|---|
| | | | | |

Name

Address

Telephone Number

E-mail Address

Gift

| Save The Day Card Sent | Invitation Sent | R.S.V.P Received | Thank You Sent | Number Attending |
|---|---|---|---|---|
| | | | | |

Name

Address

Telephone Number

E-mail Address

Gift

| Save The Day Card Sent | Invitation Sent | R.S.V.P Received | Thank You Sent | Number Attending |
|---|---|---|---|---|
| | | | | |

Name

Address

Telephone Number

E-mail Address

Gift

| Save The Day Card Sent | Invitation Sent | R.S.V.P Received | Thank You Sent | Number Attending |
|---|---|---|---|---|
| | | | | |

# Guest List Planner

Name

Address

Telephone Number

E-mail Address

Gift

| Save The Day Card Sent | Invitation Sent | R.S.V.P Received | Thank You Sent | Number Attending |
|---|---|---|---|---|

Name

Address

Telephone Number

E-mail Address

Gift

| Save The Day Card Sent | Invitation Sent | R.S.V.P Received | Thank You Sent | Number Attending |
|---|---|---|---|---|

Name

Address

Telephone Number

E-mail Address

Gift

| Save The Day Card Sent | Invitation Sent | R.S.V.P Received | Thank You Sent | Number Attending |
|---|---|---|---|---|

Name

Address

Telephone Number

E-mail Address

Gift

| Save The Day Card Sent | Invitation Sent | R.S.V.P Received | Thank You Sent | Number Attending |
|---|---|---|---|---|

Name

Address

Telephone Number

E-mail Address

Gift

| Save The Day Card Sent | Invitation Sent | R.S.V.P Received | Thank You Sent | Number Attending |
|---|---|---|---|---|

# Guest List Planner

Name

Address

Telephone Number

E-mail Address

Gift

| Save The Day Card Sent | Invitation Sent | R.S.V.P Received | Thank You Sent | Number Attending |
| --- | --- | --- | --- | --- |

Name

Address

Telephone Number

E-mail Address

Gift

| Save The Day Card Sent | Invitation Sent | R.S.V.P Received | Thank You Sent | Number Attending |
| --- | --- | --- | --- | --- |

Name

Address

Telephone Number

E-mail Address

Gift

| Save The Day Card Sent | Invitation Sent | R.S.V.P Received | Thank You Sent | Number Attending |
| --- | --- | --- | --- | --- |

Name

Address

Telephone Number

E-mail Address

Gift

| Save The Day Card Sent | Invitation Sent | R.S.V.P Received | Thank You Sent | Number Attending |
| --- | --- | --- | --- | --- |

Name

Address

Telephone Number

E-mail Address

Gift

| Save The Day Card Sent | Invitation Sent | R.S.V.P Received | Thank You Sent | Number Attending |
| --- | --- | --- | --- | --- |

# Guest List Planner

Name

Address

Telephone Number

E-mail Address

Gift

| Save The Day Card Sent | Invitation Sent | R.S.V.P Received | Thank You Sent | Number Attending |
| --- | --- | --- | --- | --- |

Name

Address

Telephone Number

E-mail Address

Gift

| Save The Day Card Sent | Invitation Sent | R.S.V.P Received | Thank You Sent | Number Attending |
| --- | --- | --- | --- | --- |

Name

Address

Telephone Number

E-mail Address

Gift

| Save The Day Card Sent | Invitation Sent | R.S.V.P Received | Thank You Sent | Number Attending |
| --- | --- | --- | --- | --- |

Name

Address

Telephone Number

E-mail Address

Gift

| Save The Day Card Sent | Invitation Sent | R.S.V.P Received | Thank You Sent | Number Attending |
| --- | --- | --- | --- | --- |

Name

Address

Telephone Number

E-mail Address

Gift

| Save The Day Card Sent | Invitation Sent | R.S.V.P Received | Thank You Sent | Number Attending |
| --- | --- | --- | --- | --- |

# Guest List Planner

Name

Address

Telephone Number

E-mail Address

Gift

| Save The Day Card Sent | Invitation Sent | R.S.V.P Received | Thank You Sent | Number Attending |
| --- | --- | --- | --- | --- |

Name

Address

Telephone Number

E-mail Address

Gift

| Save The Day Card Sent | Invitation Sent | R.S.V.P Received | Thank You Sent | Number Attending |
| --- | --- | --- | --- | --- |

Name

Address

Telephone Number

E-mail Address

Gift

| Save The Day Card Sent | Invitation Sent | R.S.V.P Received | Thank You Sent | Number Attending |
| --- | --- | --- | --- | --- |

Name

Address

Telephone Number

E-mail Address

Gift

| Save The Day Card Sent | Invitation Sent | R.S.V.P Received | Thank You Sent | Number Attending |
| --- | --- | --- | --- | --- |

Name

Address

Telephone Number

E-mail Address

Gift

| Save The Day Card Sent | Invitation Sent | R.S.V.P Received | Thank You Sent | Number Attending |
| --- | --- | --- | --- | --- |

# Guest List Planner

Name

Address

Telephone Number

E-mail Address

Gift

| Save The Day Card Sent | Invitation Sent | R.S.V.P Received | Thank You Sent | Number Attending |
| --- | --- | --- | --- | --- |

Name

Address

Telephone Number

E-mail Address

Gift

| Save The Day Card Sent | Invitation Sent | R.S.V.P Received | Thank You Sent | Number Attending |
| --- | --- | --- | --- | --- |

Name

Address

Telephone Number

E-mail Address

Gift

| Save The Day Card Sent | Invitation Sent | R.S.V.P Received | Thank You Sent | Number Attending |
| --- | --- | --- | --- | --- |

Name

Address

Telephone Number

E-mail Address

Gift

| Save The Day Card Sent | Invitation Sent | R.S.V.P Received | Thank You Sent | Number Attending |
| --- | --- | --- | --- | --- |

Name

Address

Telephone Number

E-mail Address

Gift

| Save The Day Card Sent | Invitation Sent | R.S.V.P Received | Thank You Sent | Number Attending |
| --- | --- | --- | --- | --- |

# Guest List Planner

Name

Address

Telephone Number

E-mail Address

Gift

| Save The Day Card Sent | Invitation Sent | R.S.V.P Received | Thank You Sent | Number Attending |
| --- | --- | --- | --- | --- |
| | | | | |

Name

Address

Telephone Number

E-mail Address

Gift

| Save The Day Card Sent | Invitation Sent | R.S.V.P Received | Thank You Sent | Number Attending |
| --- | --- | --- | --- | --- |
| | | | | |

Name

Address

Telephone Number

E-mail Address

Gift

| Save The Day Card Sent | Invitation Sent | R.S.V.P Received | Thank You Sent | Number Attending |
| --- | --- | --- | --- | --- |
| | | | | |

Name

Address

Telephone Number

E-mail Address

Gift

| Save The Day Card Sent | Invitation Sent | R.S.V.P Received | Thank You Sent | Number Attending |
| --- | --- | --- | --- | --- |
| | | | | |

Name

Address

Telephone Number

E-mail Address

Gift

| Save The Day Card Sent | Invitation Sent | R.S.V.P Received | Thank You Sent | Number Attending |
| --- | --- | --- | --- | --- |
| | | | | |

# Guest List Planner

Name

Address

Telephone Number

E-mail Address

Gift

| Save The Day Card Sent | Invitation Sent | R.S.V.P Received | Thank You Sent | Number Attending |
| --- | --- | --- | --- | --- |

Name

Address

Telephone Number

E-mail Address

Gift

| Save The Day Card Sent | Invitation Sent | R.S.V.P Received | Thank You Sent | Number Attending |
| --- | --- | --- | --- | --- |

Name

Address

Telephone Number

E-mail Address

Gift

| Save The Day Card Sent | Invitation Sent | R.S.V.P Received | Thank You Sent | Number Attending |
| --- | --- | --- | --- | --- |

Name

Address

Telephone Number

E-mail Address

Gift

| Save The Day Card Sent | Invitation Sent | R.S.V.P Received | Thank You Sent | Number Attending |
| --- | --- | --- | --- | --- |

Name

Address

Telephone Number

E-mail Address

Gift

| Save The Day Card Sent | Invitation Sent | R.S.V.P Received | Thank You Sent | Number Attending |
| --- | --- | --- | --- | --- |

# Guest List Planner

Name

Address

Telephone Number

E-mail Address

Gift

| Save The Day Card Sent | Invitation Sent | R.S.V.P Received | Thank You Sent | Number Attending |
| --- | --- | --- | --- | --- |

Name

Address

Telephone Number

E-mail Address

Gift

| Save The Day Card Sent | Invitation Sent | R.S.V.P Received | Thank You Sent | Number Attending |
| --- | --- | --- | --- | --- |

Name

Address

Telephone Number

E-mail Address

Gift

| Save The Day Card Sent | Invitation Sent | R.S.V.P Received | Thank You Sent | Number Attending |
| --- | --- | --- | --- | --- |

Name

Address

Telephone Number

E-mail Address

Gift

| Save The Day Card Sent | Invitation Sent | R.S.V.P Received | Thank You Sent | Number Attending |
| --- | --- | --- | --- | --- |

Name

Address

Telephone Number

E-mail Address

Gift

| Save The Day Card Sent | Invitation Sent | R.S.V.P Received | Thank You Sent | Number Attending |
| --- | --- | --- | --- | --- |

# Guest List Planner

Name

Address

Telephone Number

E-mail Address

Gift

| Save The Day Card Sent | Invitation Sent | R.S.V.P Received | Thank You Sent | Number Attending |
|---|---|---|---|---|

Name

Address

Telephone Number

E-mail Address

Gift

| Save The Day Card Sent | Invitation Sent | R.S.V.P Received | Thank You Sent | Number Attending |
|---|---|---|---|---|

Name

Address

Telephone Number

E-mail Address

Gift

| Save The Day Card Sent | Invitation Sent | R.S.V.P Received | Thank You Sent | Number Attending |
|---|---|---|---|---|

Name

Address

Telephone Number

E-mail Address

Gift

| Save The Day Card Sent | Invitation Sent | R.S.V.P Received | Thank You Sent | Number Attending |
|---|---|---|---|---|

Name

Address

Telephone Number

E-mail Address

Gift

| Save The Day Card Sent | Invitation Sent | R.S.V.P Received | Thank You Sent | Number Attending |
|---|---|---|---|---|

# Guest List Planner

Name

Address

Telephone Number

E-mail Address

Gift

| Save The Day Card Sent | Invitation Sent | R.S.V.P Received | Thank You Sent | Number Attending |
| --- | --- | --- | --- | --- |
| | | | | |

Name

Address

Telephone Number

E-mail Address

Gift

| Save The Day Card Sent | Invitation Sent | R.S.V.P Received | Thank You Sent | Number Attending |
| --- | --- | --- | --- | --- |
| | | | | |

Name

Address

Telephone Number

E-mail Address

Gift

| Save The Day Card Sent | Invitation Sent | R.S.V.P Received | Thank You Sent | Number Attending |
| --- | --- | --- | --- | --- |
| | | | | |

Name

Address

Telephone Number

E-mail Address

Gift

| Save The Day Card Sent | Invitation Sent | R.S.V.P Received | Thank You Sent | Number Attending |
| --- | --- | --- | --- | --- |
| | | | | |

Name

Address

Telephone Number

E-mail Address

Gift

| Save The Day Card Sent | Invitation Sent | R.S.V.P Received | Thank You Sent | Number Attending |
| --- | --- | --- | --- | --- |
| | | | | |

# Guest List Planner

Name

Address

Telephone Number

E-mail Address

Gift

| Save The Day Card Sent | Invitation Sent | R.S.V.P Received | Thank You Sent | Number Attending |
|---|---|---|---|---|

Name

Address

Telephone Number

E-mail Address

Gift

| Save The Day Card Sent | Invitation Sent | R.S.V.P Received | Thank You Sent | Number Attending |
|---|---|---|---|---|

Name

Address

Telephone Number

E-mail Address

Gift

| Save The Day Card Sent | Invitation Sent | R.S.V.P Received | Thank You Sent | Number Attending |
|---|---|---|---|---|

Name

Address

Telephone Number

E-mail Address

Gift

| Save The Day Card Sent | Invitation Sent | R.S.V.P Received | Thank You Sent | Number Attending |
|---|---|---|---|---|

Name

Address

Telephone Number

E-mail Address

Gift

| Save The Day Card Sent | Invitation Sent | R.S.V.P Received | Thank You Sent | Number Attending |
|---|---|---|---|---|

# Guest List Planner

Name

Address

Telephone Number

E-mail Address

Gift

| Save The Day Card Sent | Invitation Sent | R.S.V.P Received | Thank You Sent | Number Attending |
| --- | --- | --- | --- | --- |
| | | | | |

Name

Address

Telephone Number

E-mail Address

Gift

| Save The Day Card Sent | Invitation Sent | R.S.V.P Received | Thank You Sent | Number Attending |
| --- | --- | --- | --- | --- |
| | | | | |

Name

Address

Telephone Number

E-mail Address

Gift

| Save The Day Card Sent | Invitation Sent | R.S.V.P Received | Thank You Sent | Number Attending |
| --- | --- | --- | --- | --- |
| | | | | |

Name

Address

Telephone Number

E-mail Address

Gift

| Save The Day Card Sent | Invitation Sent | R.S.V.P Received | Thank You Sent | Number Attending |
| --- | --- | --- | --- | --- |
| | | | | |

Name

Address

Telephone Number

E-mail Address

Gift

| Save The Day Card Sent | Invitation Sent | R.S.V.P Received | Thank You Sent | Number Attending |
| --- | --- | --- | --- | --- |
| | | | | |

# Guest List Planner

Name

Address

Telephone Number

E-mail Address

Gift

| Save The Day Card Sent | Invitation Sent | R.S.V.P Received | Thank You Sent | Number Attending |
| --- | --- | --- | --- | --- |

Name

Address

Telephone Number

E-mail Address

Gift

| Save The Day Card Sent | Invitation Sent | R.S.V.P Received | Thank You Sent | Number Attending |
| --- | --- | --- | --- | --- |

Name

Address

Telephone Number

E-mail Address

Gift

| Save The Day Card Sent | Invitation Sent | R.S.V.P Received | Thank You Sent | Number Attending |
| --- | --- | --- | --- | --- |

Name

Address

Telephone Number

E-mail Address

Gift

| Save The Day Card Sent | Invitation Sent | R.S.V.P Received | Thank You Sent | Number Attending |
| --- | --- | --- | --- | --- |

Name

Address

Telephone Number

E-mail Address

Gift

| Save The Day Card Sent | Invitation Sent | R.S.V.P Received | Thank You Sent | Number Attending |
| --- | --- | --- | --- | --- |

# Guest List Planner

Name

Address

Telephone Number

E-mail Address

Gift

| Save The Day Card Sent | Invitation Sent | R.S.V.P Received | Thank You Sent | Number Attending |
| --- | --- | --- | --- | --- |

Name

Address

Telephone Number

E-mail Address

Gift

| Save The Day Card Sent | Invitation Sent | R.S.V.P Received | Thank You Sent | Number Attending |
| --- | --- | --- | --- | --- |

Name

Address

Telephone Number

E-mail Address

Gift

| Save The Day Card Sent | Invitation Sent | R.S.V.P Received | Thank You Sent | Number Attending |
| --- | --- | --- | --- | --- |

Name

Address

Telephone Number

E-mail Address

Gift

| Save The Day Card Sent | Invitation Sent | R.S.V.P Received | Thank You Sent | Number Attending |
| --- | --- | --- | --- | --- |

Name

Address

Telephone Number

E-mail Address

Gift

| Save The Day Card Sent | Invitation Sent | R.S.V.P Received | Thank You Sent | Number Attending |
| --- | --- | --- | --- | --- |

# Guest List Planner

Name

Address

Telephone Number

E-mail Address

Gift

| Save The Day Card Sent | Invitation Sent | R.S.V.P Received | Thank You Sent | Number Attending |
| --- | --- | --- | --- | --- |

Name

Address

Telephone Number

E-mail Address

Gift

| Save The Day Card Sent | Invitation Sent | R.S.V.P Received | Thank You Sent | Number Attending |
| --- | --- | --- | --- | --- |

Name

Address

Telephone Number

E-mail Address

Gift

| Save The Day Card Sent | Invitation Sent | R.S.V.P Received | Thank You Sent | Number Attending |
| --- | --- | --- | --- | --- |

Name

Address

Telephone Number

E-mail Address

Gift

| Save The Day Card Sent | Invitation Sent | R.S.V.P Received | Thank You Sent | Number Attending |
| --- | --- | --- | --- | --- |

Name

Address

Telephone Number

E-mail Address

Gift

| Save The Day Card Sent | Invitation Sent | R.S.V.P Received | Thank You Sent | Number Attending |
| --- | --- | --- | --- | --- |

# Guest List Planner

Name

Address

Telephone Number

E-mail Address

Gift

| Save The Day Card Sent | Invitation Sent | R.S.V.P Received | Thank You Sent | Number Attending |
| --- | --- | --- | --- | --- |
|  |  |  |  |  |

Name

Address

Telephone Number

E-mail Address

Gift

| Save The Day Card Sent | Invitation Sent | R.S.V.P Received | Thank You Sent | Number Attending |
| --- | --- | --- | --- | --- |
|  |  |  |  |  |

Name

Address

Telephone Number

E-mail Address

Gift

| Save The Day Card Sent | Invitation Sent | R.S.V.P Received | Thank You Sent | Number Attending |
| --- | --- | --- | --- | --- |
|  |  |  |  |  |

Name

Address

Telephone Number

E-mail Address

Gift

| Save The Day Card Sent | Invitation Sent | R.S.V.P Received | Thank You Sent | Number Attending |
| --- | --- | --- | --- | --- |
|  |  |  |  |  |

Name

Address

Telephone Number

E-mail Address

Gift

| Save The Day Card Sent | Invitation Sent | R.S.V.P Received | Thank You Sent | Number Attending |
| --- | --- | --- | --- | --- |
|  |  |  |  |  |

# Guest List Planner

Name

Address

Telephone Number

E-mail Address

Gift

| Save The Day Card Sent | Invitation Sent | R.S.V.P Received | Thank You Sent | Number Attending |
|---|---|---|---|---|

Name

Address

Telephone Number

E-mail Address

Gift

| Save The Day Card Sent | Invitation Sent | R.S.V.P Received | Thank You Sent | Number Attending |
|---|---|---|---|---|

Name

Address

Telephone Number

E-mail Address

Gift

| Save The Day Card Sent | Invitation Sent | R.S.V.P Received | Thank You Sent | Number Attending |
|---|---|---|---|---|

Name

Address

Telephone Number

E-mail Address

Gift

| Save The Day Card Sent | Invitation Sent | R.S.V.P Received | Thank You Sent | Number Attending |
|---|---|---|---|---|

Name

Address

Telephone Number

E-mail Address

Gift

| Save The Day Card Sent | Invitation Sent | R.S.V.P Received | Thank You Sent | Number Attending |
|---|---|---|---|---|

# Guest List Planner

Name

Address

Telephone Number

E-mail Address

Gift

| Save The Day Card Sent | Invitation Sent | R.S.V.P Received | Thank You Sent | Number Attending |
| --- | --- | --- | --- | --- |

Name

Address

Telephone Number

E-mail Address

Gift

| Save The Day Card Sent | Invitation Sent | R.S.V.P Received | Thank You Sent | Number Attending |
| --- | --- | --- | --- | --- |

Name

Address

Telephone Number

E-mail Address

Gift

| Save The Day Card Sent | Invitation Sent | R.S.V.P Received | Thank You Sent | Number Attending |
| --- | --- | --- | --- | --- |

Name

Address

Telephone Number

E-mail Address

Gift

| Save The Day Card Sent | Invitation Sent | R.S.V.P Received | Thank You Sent | Number Attending |
| --- | --- | --- | --- | --- |

Name

Address

Telephone Number

E-mail Address

Gift

| Save The Day Card Sent | Invitation Sent | R.S.V.P Received | Thank You Sent | Number Attending |
| --- | --- | --- | --- | --- |

# Guest List Planner

Name

Address

Telephone Number

E-mail Address

Gift

| Save The Day Card Sent | Invitation Sent | R.S.V.P Received | Thank You Sent | Number Attending |
| --- | --- | --- | --- | --- |
| | | | | |

Name

Address

Telephone Number

E-mail Address

Gift

| Save The Day Card Sent | Invitation Sent | R.S.V.P Received | Thank You Sent | Number Attending |
| --- | --- | --- | --- | --- |
| | | | | |

Name

Address

Telephone Number

E-mail Address

Gift

| Save The Day Card Sent | Invitation Sent | R.S.V.P Received | Thank You Sent | Number Attending |
| --- | --- | --- | --- | --- |
| | | | | |

Name

Address

Telephone Number

E-mail Address

Gift

| Save The Day Card Sent | Invitation Sent | R.S.V.P Received | Thank You Sent | Number Attending |
| --- | --- | --- | --- | --- |
| | | | | |

Name

Address

Telephone Number

E-mail Address

Gift

| Save The Day Card Sent | Invitation Sent | R.S.V.P Received | Thank You Sent | Number Attending |
| --- | --- | --- | --- | --- |
| | | | | |

# Guest List Planner

Name

Address

Telephone Number

E-mail Address

Gift

| Save The Day Card Sent | Invitation Sent | R.S.V.P Received | Thank You Sent | Number Attending |
|---|---|---|---|---|

Name

Address

Telephone Number

E-mail Address

Gift

| Save The Day Card Sent | Invitation Sent | R.S.V.P Received | Thank You Sent | Number Attending |
|---|---|---|---|---|

Name

Address

Telephone Number

E-mail Address

Gift

| Save The Day Card Sent | Invitation Sent | R.S.V.P Received | Thank You Sent | Number Attending |
|---|---|---|---|---|

Name

Address

Telephone Number

E-mail Address

Gift

| Save The Day Card Sent | Invitation Sent | R.S.V.P Received | Thank You Sent | Number Attending |
|---|---|---|---|---|

Name

Address

Telephone Number

E-mail Address

Gift

| Save The Day Card Sent | Invitation Sent | R.S.V.P Received | Thank You Sent | Number Attending |
|---|---|---|---|---|

# Guest List Planner

Name

Address

Telephone Number

E-mail Address

Gift

| Save The Day Card Sent | Invitation Sent | R.S.V.P Received | Thank You Sent | Number Attending |
| --- | --- | --- | --- | --- |

Name

Address

Telephone Number

E-mail Address

Gift

| Save The Day Card Sent | Invitation Sent | R.S.V.P Received | Thank You Sent | Number Attending |
| --- | --- | --- | --- | --- |

Name

Address

Telephone Number

E-mail Address

Gift

| Save The Day Card Sent | Invitation Sent | R.S.V.P Received | Thank You Sent | Number Attending |
| --- | --- | --- | --- | --- |

Name

Address

Telephone Number

E-mail Address

Gift

| Save The Day Card Sent | Invitation Sent | R.S.V.P Received | Thank You Sent | Number Attending |
| --- | --- | --- | --- | --- |

Name

Address

Telephone Number

E-mail Address

Gift

| Save The Day Card Sent | Invitation Sent | R.S.V.P Received | Thank You Sent | Number Attending |
| --- | --- | --- | --- | --- |

# Guest List Planner

Name

Address

Telephone Number

E-mail Address

Gift

| Save The Day Card Sent | Invitation Sent | R.S.V.P Received | Thank You Sent | Number Attending |
| --- | --- | --- | --- | --- |

Name

Address

Telephone Number

E-mail Address

Gift

| Save The Day Card Sent | Invitation Sent | R.S.V.P Received | Thank You Sent | Number Attending |
| --- | --- | --- | --- | --- |

Name

Address

Telephone Number

E-mail Address

Gift

| Save The Day Card Sent | Invitation Sent | R.S.V.P Received | Thank You Sent | Number Attending |
| --- | --- | --- | --- | --- |

Name

Address

Telephone Number

E-mail Address

Gift

| Save The Day Card Sent | Invitation Sent | R.S.V.P Received | Thank You Sent | Number Attending |
| --- | --- | --- | --- | --- |

Name

Address

Telephone Number

E-mail Address

Gift

| Save The Day Card Sent | Invitation Sent | R.S.V.P Received | Thank You Sent | Number Attending |
| --- | --- | --- | --- | --- |

# Guest List Planner

Name

Address

Telephone Number

E-mail Address

Gift

| Save The Day Card Sent | Invitation Sent | R.S.V.P Received | Thank You Sent | Number Attending |
| --- | --- | --- | --- | --- |

Name

Address

Telephone Number

E-mail Address

Gift

| Save The Day Card Sent | Invitation Sent | R.S.V.P Received | Thank You Sent | Number Attending |
| --- | --- | --- | --- | --- |

Name

Address

Telephone Number

E-mail Address

Gift

| Save The Day Card Sent | Invitation Sent | R.S.V.P Received | Thank You Sent | Number Attending |
| --- | --- | --- | --- | --- |

Name

Address

Telephone Number

E-mail Address

Gift

| Save The Day Card Sent | Invitation Sent | R.S.V.P Received | Thank You Sent | Number Attending |
| --- | --- | --- | --- | --- |

Name

Address

Telephone Number

E-mail Address

Gift

| Save The Day Card Sent | Invitation Sent | R.S.V.P Received | Thank You Sent | Number Attending |
| --- | --- | --- | --- | --- |

# Guest List Planner

Name

Address

Telephone Number

E-mail Address

Gift

| Save The Day Card Sent | Invitation Sent | R.S.V.P Received | Thank You Sent | Number Attending |
| --- | --- | --- | --- | --- |
|  |  |  |  |  |

Name

Address

Telephone Number

E-mail Address

Gift

| Save The Day Card Sent | Invitation Sent | R.S.V.P Received | Thank You Sent | Number Attending |
| --- | --- | --- | --- | --- |
|  |  |  |  |  |

Name

Address

Telephone Number

E-mail Address

Gift

| Save The Day Card Sent | Invitation Sent | R.S.V.P Received | Thank You Sent | Number Attending |
| --- | --- | --- | --- | --- |
|  |  |  |  |  |

Name

Address

Telephone Number

E-mail Address

Gift

| Save The Day Card Sent | Invitation Sent | R.S.V.P Received | Thank You Sent | Number Attending |
| --- | --- | --- | --- | --- |
|  |  |  |  |  |

Name

Address

Telephone Number

E-mail Address

Gift

| Save The Day Card Sent | Invitation Sent | R.S.V.P Received | Thank You Sent | Number Attending |
| --- | --- | --- | --- | --- |
|  |  |  |  |  |

# Guest List Planner

Name

Address

Telephone Number

E-mail Address

Gift

| Save The Day Card Sent | Invitation Sent | R.S.V.P Received | Thank You Sent | Number Attending |
| --- | --- | --- | --- | --- |

Name

Address

Telephone Number

E-mail Address

Gift

| Save The Day Card Sent | Invitation Sent | R.S.V.P Received | Thank You Sent | Number Attending |
| --- | --- | --- | --- | --- |

Name

Address

Telephone Number

E-mail Address

Gift

| Save The Day Card Sent | Invitation Sent | R.S.V.P Received | Thank You Sent | Number Attending |
| --- | --- | --- | --- | --- |

Name

Address

Telephone Number

E-mail Address

Gift

| Save The Day Card Sent | Invitation Sent | R.S.V.P Received | Thank You Sent | Number Attending |
| --- | --- | --- | --- | --- |

Name

Address

Telephone Number

E-mail Address

Gift

| Save The Day Card Sent | Invitation Sent | R.S.V.P Received | Thank You Sent | Number Attending |
| --- | --- | --- | --- | --- |

# Guest List Planner

Name

Address

Telephone Number

E-mail Address

Gift

| Save The Day Card Sent | Invitation Sent | R.S.V.P Received | Thank You Sent | Number Attending |
|---|---|---|---|---|
| | | | | |

Name

Address

Telephone Number

E-mail Address

Gift

| Save The Day Card Sent | Invitation Sent | R.S.V.P Received | Thank You Sent | Number Attending |
|---|---|---|---|---|
| | | | | |

Name

Address

Telephone Number

E-mail Address

Gift

| Save The Day Card Sent | Invitation Sent | R.S.V.P Received | Thank You Sent | Number Attending |
|---|---|---|---|---|
| | | | | |

Name

Address

Telephone Number

E-mail Address

Gift

| Save The Day Card Sent | Invitation Sent | R.S.V.P Received | Thank You Sent | Number Attending |
|---|---|---|---|---|
| | | | | |

Name

Address

Telephone Number

E-mail Address

Gift

| Save The Day Card Sent | Invitation Sent | R.S.V.P Received | Thank You Sent | Number Attending |
|---|---|---|---|---|
| | | | | |

# Guest List Planner

Name

Address

Telephone Number

E-mail Address

Gift

| Save The Day Card Sent | Invitation Sent | R.S.V.P Received | Thank You Sent | Number Attending |
|---|---|---|---|---|

Name

Address

Telephone Number

E-mail Address

Gift

| Save The Day Card Sent | Invitation Sent | R.S.V.P Received | Thank You Sent | Number Attending |
|---|---|---|---|---|

Name

Address

Telephone Number

E-mail Address

Gift

| Save The Day Card Sent | Invitation Sent | R.S.V.P Received | Thank You Sent | Number Attending |
|---|---|---|---|---|

Name

Address

Telephone Number

E-mail Address

Gift

| Save The Day Card Sent | Invitation Sent | R.S.V.P Received | Thank You Sent | Number Attending |
|---|---|---|---|---|

Name

Address

Telephone Number

E-mail Address

Gift

| Save The Day Card Sent | Invitation Sent | R.S.V.P Received | Thank You Sent | Number Attending |
|---|---|---|---|---|

# Guest List Planner

Name

Address

Telephone Number

E-mail Address

Gift

| Save The Day Card Sent | Invitation Sent | R.S.V.P Received | Thank You Sent | Number Attending |
| --- | --- | --- | --- | --- |

Name

Address

Telephone Number

E-mail Address

Gift

| Save The Day Card Sent | Invitation Sent | R.S.V.P Received | Thank You Sent | Number Attending |
| --- | --- | --- | --- | --- |

Name

Address

Telephone Number

E-mail Address

Gift

| Save The Day Card Sent | Invitation Sent | R.S.V.P Received | Thank You Sent | Number Attending |
| --- | --- | --- | --- | --- |

Name

Address

Telephone Number

E-mail Address

Gift

| Save The Day Card Sent | Invitation Sent | R.S.V.P Received | Thank You Sent | Number Attending |
| --- | --- | --- | --- | --- |

Name

Address

Telephone Number

E-mail Address

Gift

| Save The Day Card Sent | Invitation Sent | R.S.V.P Received | Thank You Sent | Number Attending |
| --- | --- | --- | --- | --- |

# Guest List Planner

Name

Address

Telephone Number

E-mail Address

Gift

| Save The Day Card Sent | Invitation Sent | R.S.V.P Received | Thank You Sent | Number Attending |
| --- | --- | --- | --- | --- |

Name

Address

Telephone Number

E-mail Address

Gift

| Save The Day Card Sent | Invitation Sent | R.S.V.P Received | Thank You Sent | Number Attending |
| --- | --- | --- | --- | --- |

Name

Address

Telephone Number

E-mail Address

Gift

| Save The Day Card Sent | Invitation Sent | R.S.V.P Received | Thank You Sent | Number Attending |
| --- | --- | --- | --- | --- |

Name

Address

Telephone Number

E-mail Address

Gift

| Save The Day Card Sent | Invitation Sent | R.S.V.P Received | Thank You Sent | Number Attending |
| --- | --- | --- | --- | --- |

Name

Address

Telephone Number

E-mail Address

Gift

| Save The Day Card Sent | Invitation Sent | R.S.V.P Received | Thank You Sent | Number Attending |
| --- | --- | --- | --- | --- |

# Guest List Planner

Name

Address

Telephone Number

E-mail Address

Gift

| Save The Day Card Sent | Invitation Sent | R.S.V.P Received | Thank You Sent | Number Attending |
| --- | --- | --- | --- | --- |
| | | | | |

Name

Address

Telephone Number

E-mail Address

Gift

| Save The Day Card Sent | Invitation Sent | R.S.V.P Received | Thank You Sent | Number Attending |
| --- | --- | --- | --- | --- |
| | | | | |

Name

Address

Telephone Number

E-mail Address

Gift

| Save The Day Card Sent | Invitation Sent | R.S.V.P Received | Thank You Sent | Number Attending |
| --- | --- | --- | --- | --- |
| | | | | |

Name

Address

Telephone Number

E-mail Address

Gift

| Save The Day Card Sent | Invitation Sent | R.S.V.P Received | Thank You Sent | Number Attending |
| --- | --- | --- | --- | --- |
| | | | | |

Name

Address

Telephone Number

E-mail Address

Gift

| Save The Day Card Sent | Invitation Sent | R.S.V.P Received | Thank You Sent | Number Attending |
| --- | --- | --- | --- | --- |
| | | | | |

# Guest List Planner

Name

Address

Telephone Number

E-mail Address

Gift

| Save The Day Card Sent | Invitation Sent | R.S.V.P Received | Thank You Sent | Number Attending |
| --- | --- | --- | --- | --- |
| | | | | |

Name

Address

Telephone Number

E-mail Address

Gift

| Save The Day Card Sent | Invitation Sent | R.S.V.P Received | Thank You Sent | Number Attending |
| --- | --- | --- | --- | --- |
| | | | | |

Name

Address

Telephone Number

E-mail Address

Gift

| Save The Day Card Sent | Invitation Sent | R.S.V.P Received | Thank You Sent | Number Attending |
| --- | --- | --- | --- | --- |
| | | | | |

Name

Address

Telephone Number

E-mail Address

Gift

| Save The Day Card Sent | Invitation Sent | R.S.V.P Received | Thank You Sent | Number Attending |
| --- | --- | --- | --- | --- |
| | | | | |

Name

Address

Telephone Number

E-mail Address

Gift

| Save The Day Card Sent | Invitation Sent | R.S.V.P Received | Thank You Sent | Number Attending |
| --- | --- | --- | --- | --- |
| | | | | |

# Guest List Planner

Name

Address

Telephone Number

E-mail Address

Gift

| Save The Day Card Sent | Invitation Sent | R.S.V.P Received | Thank You Sent | Number Attending |
| --- | --- | --- | --- | --- |
| | | | | |

Name

Address

Telephone Number

E-mail Address

Gift

| Save The Day Card Sent | Invitation Sent | R.S.V.P Received | Thank You Sent | Number Attending |
| --- | --- | --- | --- | --- |
| | | | | |

Name

Address

Telephone Number

E-mail Address

Gift

| Save The Day Card Sent | Invitation Sent | R.S.V.P Received | Thank You Sent | Number Attending |
| --- | --- | --- | --- | --- |
| | | | | |

Name

Address

Telephone Number

E-mail Address

Gift

| Save The Day Card Sent | Invitation Sent | R.S.V.P Received | Thank You Sent | Number Attending |
| --- | --- | --- | --- | --- |
| | | | | |

Name

Address

Telephone Number

E-mail Address

Gift

| Save The Day Card Sent | Invitation Sent | R.S.V.P Received | Thank You Sent | Number Attending |
| --- | --- | --- | --- | --- |
| | | | | |

# Guest List Planner

Name

Address

Telephone Number

E-mail Address

Gift

| Save The Day Card Sent | Invitation Sent | R.S.V.P Received | Thank You Sent | Number Attending |
| --- | --- | --- | --- | --- |

Name

Address

Telephone Number

E-mail Address

Gift

| Save The Day Card Sent | Invitation Sent | R.S.V.P Received | Thank You Sent | Number Attending |
| --- | --- | --- | --- | --- |

Name

Address

Telephone Number

E-mail Address

Gift

| Save The Day Card Sent | Invitation Sent | R.S.V.P Received | Thank You Sent | Number Attending |
| --- | --- | --- | --- | --- |

Name

Address

Telephone Number

E-mail Address

Gift

| Save The Day Card Sent | Invitation Sent | R.S.V.P Received | Thank You Sent | Number Attending |
| --- | --- | --- | --- | --- |

Name

Address

Telephone Number

E-mail Address

Gift

| Save The Day Card Sent | Invitation Sent | R.S.V.P Received | Thank You Sent | Number Attending |
| --- | --- | --- | --- | --- |

# Guest List Planner

Name

Address

Telephone Number

E-mail Address

Gift

| Save The Day Card Sent | Invitation Sent | R.S.V.P Received | Thank You Sent | Number Attending |
| --- | --- | --- | --- | --- |
|  |  |  |  |  |

Name

Address

Telephone Number

E-mail Address

Gift

| Save The Day Card Sent | Invitation Sent | R.S.V.P Received | Thank You Sent | Number Attending |
| --- | --- | --- | --- | --- |
|  |  |  |  |  |

Name

Address

Telephone Number

E-mail Address

Gift

| Save The Day Card Sent | Invitation Sent | R.S.V.P Received | Thank You Sent | Number Attending |
| --- | --- | --- | --- | --- |
|  |  |  |  |  |

Name

Address

Telephone Number

E-mail Address

Gift

| Save The Day Card Sent | Invitation Sent | R.S.V.P Received | Thank You Sent | Number Attending |
| --- | --- | --- | --- | --- |
|  |  |  |  |  |

Name

Address

Telephone Number

E-mail Address

Gift

| Save The Day Card Sent | Invitation Sent | R.S.V.P Received | Thank You Sent | Number Attending |
| --- | --- | --- | --- | --- |
|  |  |  |  |  |

# Guest List Planner

Name

Address

Telephone Number

E-mail Address

Gift

| Save The Day Card Sent | Invitation Sent | R.S.V.P Received | Thank You Sent | Number Attending |
| --- | --- | --- | --- | --- |

Name

Address

Telephone Number

E-mail Address

Gift

| Save The Day Card Sent | Invitation Sent | R.S.V.P Received | Thank You Sent | Number Attending |
| --- | --- | --- | --- | --- |

Name

Address

Telephone Number

E-mail Address

Gift

| Save The Day Card Sent | Invitation Sent | R.S.V.P Received | Thank You Sent | Number Attending |
| --- | --- | --- | --- | --- |

Name

Address

Telephone Number

E-mail Address

Gift

| Save The Day Card Sent | Invitation Sent | R.S.V.P Received | Thank You Sent | Number Attending |
| --- | --- | --- | --- | --- |

Name

Address

Telephone Number

E-mail Address

Gift

| Save The Day Card Sent | Invitation Sent | R.S.V.P Received | Thank You Sent | Number Attending |
| --- | --- | --- | --- | --- |

# Guest List Planner

Name

Address

Telephone Number

E-mail Address

Gift

| Save The Day Card Sent | Invitation Sent | R.S.V.P Received | Thank You Sent | Number Attending |
| --- | --- | --- | --- | --- |
|  |  |  |  |  |

Name

Address

Telephone Number

E-mail Address

Gift

| Save The Day Card Sent | Invitation Sent | R.S.V.P Received | Thank You Sent | Number Attending |
| --- | --- | --- | --- | --- |
|  |  |  |  |  |

Name

Address

Telephone Number

E-mail Address

Gift

| Save The Day Card Sent | Invitation Sent | R.S.V.P Received | Thank You Sent | Number Attending |
| --- | --- | --- | --- | --- |
|  |  |  |  |  |

Name

Address

Telephone Number

E-mail Address

Gift

| Save The Day Card Sent | Invitation Sent | R.S.V.P Received | Thank You Sent | Number Attending |
| --- | --- | --- | --- | --- |
|  |  |  |  |  |

Name

Address

Telephone Number

E-mail Address

Gift

| Save The Day Card Sent | Invitation Sent | R.S.V.P Received | Thank You Sent | Number Attending |
| --- | --- | --- | --- | --- |
|  |  |  |  |  |

# Guest List Planner

Name

Address

Telephone Number

E-mail Address

Gift

| Save The Day Card Sent | Invitation Sent | R.S.V.P Received | Thank You Sent | Number Attending |
| --- | --- | --- | --- | --- |

Name

Address

Telephone Number

E-mail Address

Gift

| Save The Day Card Sent | Invitation Sent | R.S.V.P Received | Thank You Sent | Number Attending |
| --- | --- | --- | --- | --- |

Name

Address

Telephone Number

E-mail Address

Gift

| Save The Day Card Sent | Invitation Sent | R.S.V.P Received | Thank You Sent | Number Attending |
| --- | --- | --- | --- | --- |

Name

Address

Telephone Number

E-mail Address

Gift

| Save The Day Card Sent | Invitation Sent | R.S.V.P Received | Thank You Sent | Number Attending |
| --- | --- | --- | --- | --- |

Name

Address

Telephone Number

E-mail Address

Gift

| Save The Day Card Sent | Invitation Sent | R.S.V.P Received | Thank You Sent | Number Attending |
| --- | --- | --- | --- | --- |

# Guest List Planner

Name
_______________________________________________

Address
_______________________________________________

Telephone Number
_______________________________________________

E-mail Address
_______________________________________________

Gift
_______________________________________________

| Save The Day Card Sent | Invitation Sent | R.S.V.P Received | Thank You Sent | Number Attending |
| --- | --- | --- | --- | --- |
| | | | | |

Name
_______________________________________________

Address
_______________________________________________

Telephone Number
_______________________________________________

E-mail Address
_______________________________________________

Gift
_______________________________________________

| Save The Day Card Sent | Invitation Sent | R.S.V.P Received | Thank You Sent | Number Attending |
| --- | --- | --- | --- | --- |
| | | | | |

Name
_______________________________________________

Address
_______________________________________________

Telephone Number
_______________________________________________

E-mail Address
_______________________________________________

Gift
_______________________________________________

| Save The Day Card Sent | Invitation Sent | R.S.V.P Received | Thank You Sent | Number Attending |
| --- | --- | --- | --- | --- |
| | | | | |

Name
_______________________________________________

Address
_______________________________________________

Telephone Number
_______________________________________________

E-mail Address
_______________________________________________

Gift
_______________________________________________

| Save The Day Card Sent | Invitation Sent | R.S.V.P Received | Thank You Sent | Number Attending |
| --- | --- | --- | --- | --- |
| | | | | |

Name
_______________________________________________

Address
_______________________________________________

Telephone Number
_______________________________________________

E-mail Address
_______________________________________________

Gift
_______________________________________________

| Save The Day Card Sent | Invitation Sent | R.S.V.P Received | Thank You Sent | Number Attending |
| --- | --- | --- | --- | --- |
| | | | | |

# Guest List Planner

Name

Address

Telephone Number

E-mail Address

Gift

| Save The Day Card Sent | Invitation Sent | R.S.V.P Received | Thank You Sent | Number Attending |
| --- | --- | --- | --- | --- |

Name

Address

Telephone Number

E-mail Address

Gift

| Save The Day Card Sent | Invitation Sent | R.S.V.P Received | Thank You Sent | Number Attending |
| --- | --- | --- | --- | --- |

Name

Address

Telephone Number

E-mail Address

Gift

| Save The Day Card Sent | Invitation Sent | R.S.V.P Received | Thank You Sent | Number Attending |
| --- | --- | --- | --- | --- |

Name

Address

Telephone Number

E-mail Address

Gift

| Save The Day Card Sent | Invitation Sent | R.S.V.P Received | Thank You Sent | Number Attending |
| --- | --- | --- | --- | --- |

Name

Address

Telephone Number

E-mail Address

Gift

| Save The Day Card Sent | Invitation Sent | R.S.V.P Received | Thank You Sent | Number Attending |
| --- | --- | --- | --- | --- |

# Guest List Planner

Name

Address

Telephone Number

E-mail Address

Gift

| Save The Day Card Sent | Invitation Sent | R.S.V.P Received | Thank You Sent | Number Attending |
|---|---|---|---|---|

Name

Address

Telephone Number

E-mail Address

Gift

| Save The Day Card Sent | Invitation Sent | R.S.V.P Received | Thank You Sent | Number Attending |
|---|---|---|---|---|

Name

Address

Telephone Number

E-mail Address

Gift

| Save The Day Card Sent | Invitation Sent | R.S.V.P Received | Thank You Sent | Number Attending |
|---|---|---|---|---|

Name

Address

Telephone Number

E-mail Address

Gift

| Save The Day Card Sent | Invitation Sent | R.S.V.P Received | Thank You Sent | Number Attending |
|---|---|---|---|---|

Name

Address

Telephone Number

E-mail Address

Gift

| Save The Day Card Sent | Invitation Sent | R.S.V.P Received | Thank You Sent | Number Attending |
|---|---|---|---|---|

# Guest List Planner

Name

Address

Telephone Number

E-mail Address

Gift

| Save The Day Card Sent | Invitation Sent | R.S.V.P Received | Thank You Sent | Number Attending |
| --- | --- | --- | --- | --- |

Name

Address

Telephone Number

E-mail Address

Gift

| Save The Day Card Sent | Invitation Sent | R.S.V.P Received | Thank You Sent | Number Attending |
| --- | --- | --- | --- | --- |

Name

Address

Telephone Number

E-mail Address

Gift

| Save The Day Card Sent | Invitation Sent | R.S.V.P Received | Thank You Sent | Number Attending |
| --- | --- | --- | --- | --- |

Name

Address

Telephone Number

E-mail Address

Gift

| Save The Day Card Sent | Invitation Sent | R.S.V.P Received | Thank You Sent | Number Attending |
| --- | --- | --- | --- | --- |

Name

Address

Telephone Number

E-mail Address

Gift

| Save The Day Card Sent | Invitation Sent | R.S.V.P Received | Thank You Sent | Number Attending |
| --- | --- | --- | --- | --- |

# Guest List Planner

Name

Address

Telephone Number

E-mail Address

Gift

| Save The Day Card Sent | Invitation Sent | R.S.V.P Received | Thank You Sent | Number Attending |
| --- | --- | --- | --- | --- |
| | | | | |

Name

Address

Telephone Number

E-mail Address

Gift

| Save The Day Card Sent | Invitation Sent | R.S.V.P Received | Thank You Sent | Number Attending |
| --- | --- | --- | --- | --- |
| | | | | |

Name

Address

Telephone Number

E-mail Address

Gift

| Save The Day Card Sent | Invitation Sent | R.S.V.P Received | Thank You Sent | Number Attending |
| --- | --- | --- | --- | --- |
| | | | | |

Name

Address

Telephone Number

E-mail Address

Gift

| Save The Day Card Sent | Invitation Sent | R.S.V.P Received | Thank You Sent | Number Attending |
| --- | --- | --- | --- | --- |
| | | | | |

Name

Address

Telephone Number

E-mail Address

Gift

| Save The Day Card Sent | Invitation Sent | R.S.V.P Received | Thank You Sent | Number Attending |
| --- | --- | --- | --- | --- |
| | | | | |

# Guest List Planner

Name

Address

Telephone Number

E-mail Address

Gift

| Save The Day Card Sent | Invitation Sent | R.S.V.P Received | Thank You Sent | Number Attending |
| --- | --- | --- | --- | --- |

Name

Address

Telephone Number

E-mail Address

Gift

| Save The Day Card Sent | Invitation Sent | R.S.V.P Received | Thank You Sent | Number Attending |
| --- | --- | --- | --- | --- |

Name

Address

Telephone Number

E-mail Address

Gift

| Save The Day Card Sent | Invitation Sent | R.S.V.P Received | Thank You Sent | Number Attending |
| --- | --- | --- | --- | --- |

Name

Address

Telephone Number

E-mail Address

Gift

| Save The Day Card Sent | Invitation Sent | R.S.V.P Received | Thank You Sent | Number Attending |
| --- | --- | --- | --- | --- |

Name

Address

Telephone Number

E-mail Address

Gift

| Save The Day Card Sent | Invitation Sent | R.S.V.P Received | Thank You Sent | Number Attending |
| --- | --- | --- | --- | --- |

# Guest List Planner

Name

Address

Telephone Number

E-mail Address

Gift

| Save The Day Card Sent | Invitation Sent | R.S.V.P Received | Thank You Sent | Number Attending |
| --- | --- | --- | --- | --- |
| | | | | |

Name

Address

Telephone Number

E-mail Address

Gift

| Save The Day Card Sent | Invitation Sent | R.S.V.P Received | Thank You Sent | Number Attending |
| --- | --- | --- | --- | --- |
| | | | | |

Name

Address

Telephone Number

E-mail Address

Gift

| Save The Day Card Sent | Invitation Sent | R.S.V.P Received | Thank You Sent | Number Attending |
| --- | --- | --- | --- | --- |
| | | | | |

Name

Address

Telephone Number

E-mail Address

Gift

| Save The Day Card Sent | Invitation Sent | R.S.V.P Received | Thank You Sent | Number Attending |
| --- | --- | --- | --- | --- |
| | | | | |

Name

Address

Telephone Number

E-mail Address

Gift

| Save The Day Card Sent | Invitation Sent | R.S.V.P Received | Thank You Sent | Number Attending |
| --- | --- | --- | --- | --- |
| | | | | |

# Guest List Planner

Name

Address

Telephone Number

E-mail Address

Gift

| Save The Day Card Sent | Invitation Sent | R.S.V.P Received | Thank You Sent | Number Attending |
| --- | --- | --- | --- | --- |

Name

Address

Telephone Number

E-mail Address

Gift

| Save The Day Card Sent | Invitation Sent | R.S.V.P Received | Thank You Sent | Number Attending |
| --- | --- | --- | --- | --- |

Name

Address

Telephone Number

E-mail Address

Gift

| Save The Day Card Sent | Invitation Sent | R.S.V.P Received | Thank You Sent | Number Attending |
| --- | --- | --- | --- | --- |

Name

Address

Telephone Number

E-mail Address

Gift

| Save The Day Card Sent | Invitation Sent | R.S.V.P Received | Thank You Sent | Number Attending |
| --- | --- | --- | --- | --- |

Name

Address

Telephone Number

E-mail Address

Gift

| Save The Day Card Sent | Invitation Sent | R.S.V.P Received | Thank You Sent | Number Attending |
| --- | --- | --- | --- | --- |

# *Guest List Planner*

Name

Address

Telephone Number

E-mail Address

Gift

| Save The Day<br>Card Sent | Invitation<br>Sent | R.S.V.P<br>Received | Thank You<br>Sent | Number<br>Attending |
| --- | --- | --- | --- | --- |

Name

Address

Telephone Number

E-mail Address

Gift

| Save The Day<br>Card Sent | Invitation<br>Sent | R.S.V.P<br>Received | Thank You<br>Sent | Number<br>Attending |
| --- | --- | --- | --- | --- |

Name

Address

Telephone Number

E-mail Address

Gift

| Save The Day<br>Card Sent | Invitation<br>Sent | R.S.V.P<br>Received | Thank You<br>Sent | Number<br>Attending |
| --- | --- | --- | --- | --- |

Name

Address

Telephone Number

E-mail Address

Gift

| Save The Day<br>Card Sent | Invitation<br>Sent | R.S.V.P<br>Received | Thank You<br>Sent | Number<br>Attending |
| --- | --- | --- | --- | --- |

Name

Address

Telephone Number

E-mail Address

Gift

| Save The Day<br>Card Sent | Invitation<br>Sent | R.S.V.P<br>Received | Thank You<br>Sent | Number<br>Attending |
| --- | --- | --- | --- | --- |

# Guest List Planner

Name

Address

Telephone Number

E-mail Address

Gift

| Save The Day Card Sent | Invitation Sent | R.S.V.P Received | Thank You Sent | Number Attending |
| --- | --- | --- | --- | --- |
| | | | | |

Name

Address

Telephone Number

E-mail Address

Gift

| Save The Day Card Sent | Invitation Sent | R.S.V.P Received | Thank You Sent | Number Attending |
| --- | --- | --- | --- | --- |
| | | | | |

Name

Address

Telephone Number

E-mail Address

Gift

| Save The Day Card Sent | Invitation Sent | R.S.V.P Received | Thank You Sent | Number Attending |
| --- | --- | --- | --- | --- |
| | | | | |

Name

Address

Telephone Number

E-mail Address

Gift

| Save The Day Card Sent | Invitation Sent | R.S.V.P Received | Thank You Sent | Number Attending |
| --- | --- | --- | --- | --- |
| | | | | |

Name

Address

Telephone Number

E-mail Address

Gift

| Save The Day Card Sent | Invitation Sent | R.S.V.P Received | Thank You Sent | Number Attending |
| --- | --- | --- | --- | --- |
| | | | | |

# Guest List Planner

Name

Address

Telephone Number

E-mail Address

Gift

| Save The Day Card Sent | Invitation Sent | R.S.V.P Received | Thank You Sent | Number Attending |
| --- | --- | --- | --- | --- |
| | | | | |

Name

Address

Telephone Number

E-mail Address

Gift

| Save The Day Card Sent | Invitation Sent | R.S.V.P Received | Thank You Sent | Number Attending |
| --- | --- | --- | --- | --- |
| | | | | |

Name

Address

Telephone Number

E-mail Address

Gift

| Save The Day Card Sent | Invitation Sent | R.S.V.P Received | Thank You Sent | Number Attending |
| --- | --- | --- | --- | --- |
| | | | | |

Name

Address

Telephone Number

E-mail Address

Gift

| Save The Day Card Sent | Invitation Sent | R.S.V.P Received | Thank You Sent | Number Attending |
| --- | --- | --- | --- | --- |
| | | | | |

Name

Address

Telephone Number

E-mail Address

Gift

| Save The Day Card Sent | Invitation Sent | R.S.V.P Received | Thank You Sent | Number Attending |
| --- | --- | --- | --- | --- |
| | | | | |

# Guest List Planner

Name

Address

Telephone Number

E-mail Address

Gift

| Save The Day Card Sent | Invitation Sent | R.S.V.P Received | Thank You Sent | Number Attending |
| --- | --- | --- | --- | --- |

Name

Address

Telephone Number

E-mail Address

Gift

| Save The Day Card Sent | Invitation Sent | R.S.V.P Received | Thank You Sent | Number Attending |
| --- | --- | --- | --- | --- |

Name

Address

Telephone Number

E-mail Address

Gift

| Save The Day Card Sent | Invitation Sent | R.S.V.P Received | Thank You Sent | Number Attending |
| --- | --- | --- | --- | --- |

Name

Address

Telephone Number

E-mail Address

Gift

| Save The Day Card Sent | Invitation Sent | R.S.V.P Received | Thank You Sent | Number Attending |
| --- | --- | --- | --- | --- |

Name

Address

Telephone Number

E-mail Address

Gift

| Save The Day Card Sent | Invitation Sent | R.S.V.P Received | Thank You Sent | Number Attending |
| --- | --- | --- | --- | --- |

# Guest List Planner

Name

Address

Telephone Number

E-mail Address

Gift

| Save The Day Card Sent | Invitation Sent | R.S.V.P Received | Thank You Sent | Number Attending |
| --- | --- | --- | --- | --- |

Name

Address

Telephone Number

E-mail Address

Gift

| Save The Day Card Sent | Invitation Sent | R.S.V.P Received | Thank You Sent | Number Attending |
| --- | --- | --- | --- | --- |

Name

Address

Telephone Number

E-mail Address

Gift

| Save The Day Card Sent | Invitation Sent | R.S.V.P Received | Thank You Sent | Number Attending |
| --- | --- | --- | --- | --- |

Name

Address

Telephone Number

E-mail Address

Gift

| Save The Day Card Sent | Invitation Sent | R.S.V.P Received | Thank You Sent | Number Attending |
| --- | --- | --- | --- | --- |

Name

Address

Telephone Number

E-mail Address

Gift

| Save The Day Card Sent | Invitation Sent | R.S.V.P Received | Thank You Sent | Number Attending |
| --- | --- | --- | --- | --- |

# Guest List Planner

Name

Address

Telephone Number

E-mail Address

Gift

| Save The Day Card Sent | Invitation Sent | R.S.V.P Received | Thank You Sent | Number Attending |
| --- | --- | --- | --- | --- |

Name

Address

Telephone Number

E-mail Address

Gift

| Save The Day Card Sent | Invitation Sent | R.S.V.P Received | Thank You Sent | Number Attending |
| --- | --- | --- | --- | --- |

Name

Address

Telephone Number

E-mail Address

Gift

| Save The Day Card Sent | Invitation Sent | R.S.V.P Received | Thank You Sent | Number Attending |
| --- | --- | --- | --- | --- |

Name

Address

Telephone Number

E-mail Address

Gift

| Save The Day Card Sent | Invitation Sent | R.S.V.P Received | Thank You Sent | Number Attending |
| --- | --- | --- | --- | --- |

Name

Address

Telephone Number

E-mail Address

Gift

| Save The Day Card Sent | Invitation Sent | R.S.V.P Received | Thank You Sent | Number Attending |
| --- | --- | --- | --- | --- |

# Guest List Planner

Name

Address

Telephone Number

E-mail Address

Gift

| Save The Day Card Sent | Invitation Sent | R.S.V.P Received | Thank You Sent | Number Attending |
| --- | --- | --- | --- | --- |

Name

Address

Telephone Number

E-mail Address

Gift

| Save The Day Card Sent | Invitation Sent | R.S.V.P Received | Thank You Sent | Number Attending |
| --- | --- | --- | --- | --- |

Name

Address

Telephone Number

E-mail Address

Gift

| Save The Day Card Sent | Invitation Sent | R.S.V.P Received | Thank You Sent | Number Attending |
| --- | --- | --- | --- | --- |

Name

Address

Telephone Number

E-mail Address

Gift

| Save The Day Card Sent | Invitation Sent | R.S.V.P Received | Thank You Sent | Number Attending |
| --- | --- | --- | --- | --- |

Name

Address

Telephone Number

E-mail Address

Gift

| Save The Day Card Sent | Invitation Sent | R.S.V.P Received | Thank You Sent | Number Attending |
| --- | --- | --- | --- | --- |

# Guest List Planner

Name

Address

Telephone Number

E-mail Address

Gift

| Save The Day Card Sent | Invitation Sent | R.S.V.P Received | Thank You Sent | Number Attending |
| --- | --- | --- | --- | --- |

Name

Address

Telephone Number

E-mail Address

Gift

| Save The Day Card Sent | Invitation Sent | R.S.V.P Received | Thank You Sent | Number Attending |
| --- | --- | --- | --- | --- |

Name

Address

Telephone Number

E-mail Address

Gift

| Save The Day Card Sent | Invitation Sent | R.S.V.P Received | Thank You Sent | Number Attending |
| --- | --- | --- | --- | --- |

Name

Address

Telephone Number

E-mail Address

Gift

| Save The Day Card Sent | Invitation Sent | R.S.V.P Received | Thank You Sent | Number Attending |
| --- | --- | --- | --- | --- |

Name

Address

Telephone Number

E-mail Address

Gift

| Save The Day Card Sent | Invitation Sent | R.S.V.P Received | Thank You Sent | Number Attending |
| --- | --- | --- | --- | --- |

# Guest List Planner

Name

Address

Telephone Number

E-mail Address

Gift

| Save The Day Card Sent | Invitation Sent | R.S.V.P Received | Thank You Sent | Number Attending |
| --- | --- | --- | --- | --- |

Name

Address

Telephone Number

E-mail Address

Gift

| Save The Day Card Sent | Invitation Sent | R.S.V.P Received | Thank You Sent | Number Attending |
| --- | --- | --- | --- | --- |

Name

Address

Telephone Number

E-mail Address

Gift

| Save The Day Card Sent | Invitation Sent | R.S.V.P Received | Thank You Sent | Number Attending |
| --- | --- | --- | --- | --- |

Name

Address

Telephone Number

E-mail Address

Gift

| Save The Day Card Sent | Invitation Sent | R.S.V.P Received | Thank You Sent | Number Attending |
| --- | --- | --- | --- | --- |

Name

Address

Telephone Number

E-mail Address

Gift

| Save The Day Card Sent | Invitation Sent | R.S.V.P Received | Thank You Sent | Number Attending |
| --- | --- | --- | --- | --- |

# Guest List Planner

Name

Address

Telephone Number

E-mail Address

Gift

| Save The Day Card Sent | Invitation Sent | R.S.V.P Received | Thank You Sent | Number Attending |
|---|---|---|---|---|

Name

Address

Telephone Number

E-mail Address

Gift

| Save The Day Card Sent | Invitation Sent | R.S.V.P Received | Thank You Sent | Number Attending |
|---|---|---|---|---|

Name

Address

Telephone Number

E-mail Address

Gift

| Save The Day Card Sent | Invitation Sent | R.S.V.P Received | Thank You Sent | Number Attending |
|---|---|---|---|---|

Name

Address

Telephone Number

E-mail Address

Gift

| Save The Day Card Sent | Invitation Sent | R.S.V.P Received | Thank You Sent | Number Attending |
|---|---|---|---|---|

Name

Address

Telephone Number

E-mail Address

Gift

| Save The Day Card Sent | Invitation Sent | R.S.V.P Received | Thank You Sent | Number Attending |
|---|---|---|---|---|

# Guest List Planner

Name
_______________________________________

Address
_______________________________________

Telephone Number
_______________________________________

E-mail Address
_______________________________________

Gift
_______________________________________

| Save The Day Card Sent | Invitation Sent | R.S.V.P Received | Thank You Sent | Number Attending |
| --- | --- | --- | --- | --- |
| | | | | |

Name
_______________________________________

Address
_______________________________________

Telephone Number
_______________________________________

E-mail Address
_______________________________________

Gift
_______________________________________

| Save The Day Card Sent | Invitation Sent | R.S.V.P Received | Thank You Sent | Number Attending |
| --- | --- | --- | --- | --- |
| | | | | |

Name
_______________________________________

Address
_______________________________________

Telephone Number
_______________________________________

E-mail Address
_______________________________________

Gift
_______________________________________

| Save The Day Card Sent | Invitation Sent | R.S.V.P Received | Thank You Sent | Number Attending |
| --- | --- | --- | --- | --- |
| | | | | |

Name
_______________________________________

Address
_______________________________________

Telephone Number
_______________________________________

E-mail Address
_______________________________________

Gift
_______________________________________

| Save The Day Card Sent | Invitation Sent | R.S.V.P Received | Thank You Sent | Number Attending |
| --- | --- | --- | --- | --- |
| | | | | |

Name
_______________________________________

Address
_______________________________________

Telephone Number
_______________________________________

E-mail Address
_______________________________________

Gift
_______________________________________

| Save The Day Card Sent | Invitation Sent | R.S.V.P Received | Thank You Sent | Number Attending |
| --- | --- | --- | --- | --- |
| | | | | |

# Guest List Planner

Name

Address

Telephone Number

E-mail Address

Gift

| Save The Day Card Sent | Invitation Sent | R.S.V.P Received | Thank You Sent | Number Attending |
| --- | --- | --- | --- | --- |

Name

Address

Telephone Number

E-mail Address

Gift

| Save The Day Card Sent | Invitation Sent | R.S.V.P Received | Thank You Sent | Number Attending |
| --- | --- | --- | --- | --- |

Name

Address

Telephone Number

E-mail Address

Gift

| Save The Day Card Sent | Invitation Sent | R.S.V.P Received | Thank You Sent | Number Attending |
| --- | --- | --- | --- | --- |

Name

Address

Telephone Number

E-mail Address

Gift

| Save The Day Card Sent | Invitation Sent | R.S.V.P Received | Thank You Sent | Number Attending |
| --- | --- | --- | --- | --- |

Name

Address

Telephone Number

E-mail Address

Gift

| Save The Day Card Sent | Invitation Sent | R.S.V.P Received | Thank You Sent | Number Attending |
| --- | --- | --- | --- | --- |

# Guest List Planner

Name

Address

Telephone Number

E-mail Address

Gift

| Save The Day Card Sent | Invitation Sent | R.S.V.P Received | Thank You Sent | Number Attending |
| --- | --- | --- | --- | --- |

Name

Address

Telephone Number

E-mail Address

Gift

| Save The Day Card Sent | Invitation Sent | R.S.V.P Received | Thank You Sent | Number Attending |
| --- | --- | --- | --- | --- |

Name

Address

Telephone Number

E-mail Address

Gift

| Save The Day Card Sent | Invitation Sent | R.S.V.P Received | Thank You Sent | Number Attending |
| --- | --- | --- | --- | --- |

Name

Address

Telephone Number

E-mail Address

Gift

| Save The Day Card Sent | Invitation Sent | R.S.V.P Received | Thank You Sent | Number Attending |
| --- | --- | --- | --- | --- |

Name

Address

Telephone Number

E-mail Address

Gift

| Save The Day Card Sent | Invitation Sent | R.S.V.P Received | Thank You Sent | Number Attending |
| --- | --- | --- | --- | --- |

# Guest List Planner

Name

Address

Telephone Number

E-mail Address

Gift

| Save The Day Card Sent | Invitation Sent | R.S.V.P Received | Thank You Sent | Number Attending |
|---|---|---|---|---|

Name

Address

Telephone Number

E-mail Address

Gift

| Save The Day Card Sent | Invitation Sent | R.S.V.P Received | Thank You Sent | Number Attending |
|---|---|---|---|---|

Name

Address

Telephone Number

E-mail Address

Gift

| Save The Day Card Sent | Invitation Sent | R.S.V.P Received | Thank You Sent | Number Attending |
|---|---|---|---|---|

Name

Address

Telephone Number

E-mail Address

Gift

| Save The Day Card Sent | Invitation Sent | R.S.V.P Received | Thank You Sent | Number Attending |
|---|---|---|---|---|

Name

Address

Telephone Number

E-mail Address

Gift

| Save The Day Card Sent | Invitation Sent | R.S.V.P Received | Thank You Sent | Number Attending |
|---|---|---|---|---|

# Guest List Planner

Name

Address

Telephone Number

E-mail Address

Gift

| Save The Day Card Sent | Invitation Sent | R.S.V.P Received | Thank You Sent | Number Attending |
| --- | --- | --- | --- | --- |
| | | | | |

Name

Address

Telephone Number

E-mail Address

Gift

| Save The Day Card Sent | Invitation Sent | R.S.V.P Received | Thank You Sent | Number Attending |
| --- | --- | --- | --- | --- |
| | | | | |

Name

Address

Telephone Number

E-mail Address

Gift

| Save The Day Card Sent | Invitation Sent | R.S.V.P Received | Thank You Sent | Number Attending |
| --- | --- | --- | --- | --- |
| | | | | |

Name

Address

Telephone Number

E-mail Address

Gift

| Save The Day Card Sent | Invitation Sent | R.S.V.P Received | Thank You Sent | Number Attending |
| --- | --- | --- | --- | --- |
| | | | | |

Name

Address

Telephone Number

E-mail Address

Gift

| Save The Day Card Sent | Invitation Sent | R.S.V.P Received | Thank You Sent | Number Attending |
| --- | --- | --- | --- | --- |
| | | | | |

# Guest List Planner

Name

Address

Telephone Number

E-mail Address

Gift

| Save The Day Card Sent | Invitation Sent | R.S.V.P Received | Thank You Sent | Number Attending |
| --- | --- | --- | --- | --- |

Name

Address

Telephone Number

E-mail Address

Gift

| Save The Day Card Sent | Invitation Sent | R.S.V.P Received | Thank You Sent | Number Attending |
| --- | --- | --- | --- | --- |

Name

Address

Telephone Number

E-mail Address

Gift

| Save The Day Card Sent | Invitation Sent | R.S.V.P Received | Thank You Sent | Number Attending |
| --- | --- | --- | --- | --- |

Name

Address

Telephone Number

E-mail Address

Gift

| Save The Day Card Sent | Invitation Sent | R.S.V.P Received | Thank You Sent | Number Attending |
| --- | --- | --- | --- | --- |

Name

Address

Telephone Number

E-mail Address

Gift

| Save The Day Card Sent | Invitation Sent | R.S.V.P Received | Thank You Sent | Number Attending |
| --- | --- | --- | --- | --- |

# Guest List Planner

Name

Address

Telephone Number

E-mail Address

Gift

| Save The Day Card Sent | Invitation Sent | R.S.V.P Received | Thank You Sent | Number Attending |
| --- | --- | --- | --- | --- |
|  |  |  |  |  |

Name

Address

Telephone Number

E-mail Address

Gift

| Save The Day Card Sent | Invitation Sent | R.S.V.P Received | Thank You Sent | Number Attending |
| --- | --- | --- | --- | --- |
|  |  |  |  |  |

Name

Address

Telephone Number

E-mail Address

Gift

| Save The Day Card Sent | Invitation Sent | R.S.V.P Received | Thank You Sent | Number Attending |
| --- | --- | --- | --- | --- |
|  |  |  |  |  |

Name

Address

Telephone Number

E-mail Address

Gift

| Save The Day Card Sent | Invitation Sent | R.S.V.P Received | Thank You Sent | Number Attending |
| --- | --- | --- | --- | --- |
|  |  |  |  |  |

Name

Address

Telephone Number

E-mail Address

Gift

| Save The Day Card Sent | Invitation Sent | R.S.V.P Received | Thank You Sent | Number Attending |
| --- | --- | --- | --- | --- |
|  |  |  |  |  |

# Guest List Planner

Name

Address

Telephone Number

E-mail Address

Gift

| Save The Day Card Sent | Invitation Sent | R.S.V.P Received | Thank You Sent | Number Attending |
|---|---|---|---|---|

Name

Address

Telephone Number

E-mail Address

Gift

| Save The Day Card Sent | Invitation Sent | R.S.V.P Received | Thank You Sent | Number Attending |
|---|---|---|---|---|

Name

Address

Telephone Number

E-mail Address

Gift

| Save The Day Card Sent | Invitation Sent | R.S.V.P Received | Thank You Sent | Number Attending |
|---|---|---|---|---|

Name

Address

Telephone Number

E-mail Address

Gift

| Save The Day Card Sent | Invitation Sent | R.S.V.P Received | Thank You Sent | Number Attending |
|---|---|---|---|---|

Name

Address

Telephone Number

E-mail Address

Gift

| Save The Day Card Sent | Invitation Sent | R.S.V.P Received | Thank You Sent | Number Attending |
|---|---|---|---|---|

# Guest List Planner

**Name**

**Address**

**Telephone Number**

**E-mail Address**

**Gift**

| Save The Day Card Sent | Invitation Sent | R.S.V.P Received | Thank You Sent | Number Attending |
|---|---|---|---|---|
| | | | | |

**Name**

**Address**

**Telephone Number**

**E-mail Address**

**Gift**

| Save The Day Card Sent | Invitation Sent | R.S.V.P Received | Thank You Sent | Number Attending |
|---|---|---|---|---|
| | | | | |

**Name**

**Address**

**Telephone Number**

**E-mail Address**

**Gift**

| Save The Day Card Sent | Invitation Sent | R.S.V.P Received | Thank You Sent | Number Attending |
|---|---|---|---|---|
| | | | | |

**Name**

**Address**

**Telephone Number**

**E-mail Address**

**Gift**

| Save The Day Card Sent | Invitation Sent | R.S.V.P Received | Thank You Sent | Number Attending |
|---|---|---|---|---|
| | | | | |

**Name**

**Address**

**Telephone Number**

**E-mail Address**

**Gift**

| Save The Day Card Sent | Invitation Sent | R.S.V.P Received | Thank You Sent | Number Attending |
|---|---|---|---|---|
| | | | | |

# Guest List Planner

Name

Address

Telephone Number

E-mail Address

Gift

| Save The Day Card Sent | Invitation Sent | R.S.V.P Received | Thank You Sent | Number Attending |
| --- | --- | --- | --- | --- |
| | | | | |

Name

Address

Telephone Number

E-mail Address

Gift

| Save The Day Card Sent | Invitation Sent | R.S.V.P Received | Thank You Sent | Number Attending |
| --- | --- | --- | --- | --- |
| | | | | |

Name

Address

Telephone Number

E-mail Address

Gift

| Save The Day Card Sent | Invitation Sent | R.S.V.P Received | Thank You Sent | Number Attending |
| --- | --- | --- | --- | --- |
| | | | | |

Name

Address

Telephone Number

E-mail Address

Gift

| Save The Day Card Sent | Invitation Sent | R.S.V.P Received | Thank You Sent | Number Attending |
| --- | --- | --- | --- | --- |
| | | | | |

Name

Address

Telephone Number

E-mail Address

Gift

| Save The Day Card Sent | Invitation Sent | R.S.V.P Received | Thank You Sent | Number Attending |
| --- | --- | --- | --- | --- |
| | | | | |

# Guest List Planner

**Name**

**Address**

**Telephone Number**

**E-mail Address**

**Gift**

| Save The Day Card Sent | Invitation Sent | R.S.V.P Received | Thank You Sent | Number Attending |
| --- | --- | --- | --- | --- |
| | | | | |

**Name**

**Address**

**Telephone Number**

**E-mail Address**

**Gift**

| Save The Day Card Sent | Invitation Sent | R.S.V.P Received | Thank You Sent | Number Attending |
| --- | --- | --- | --- | --- |
| | | | | |

**Name**

**Address**

**Telephone Number**

**E-mail Address**

**Gift**

| Save The Day Card Sent | Invitation Sent | R.S.V.P Received | Thank You Sent | Number Attending |
| --- | --- | --- | --- | --- |
| | | | | |

**Name**

**Address**

**Telephone Number**

**E-mail Address**

**Gift**

| Save The Day Card Sent | Invitation Sent | R.S.V.P Received | Thank You Sent | Number Attending |
| --- | --- | --- | --- | --- |
| | | | | |

**Name**

**Address**

**Telephone Number**

**E-mail Address**

**Gift**

| Save The Day Card Sent | Invitation Sent | R.S.V.P Received | Thank You Sent | Number Attending |
| --- | --- | --- | --- | --- |
| | | | | |

# Guest List Planner

Name

Address

Telephone Number

E-mail Address

Gift

| Save The Day Card Sent | Invitation Sent | R.S.V.P Received | Thank You Sent | Number Attending |
| --- | --- | --- | --- | --- |

Name

Address

Telephone Number

E-mail Address

Gift

| Save The Day Card Sent | Invitation Sent | R.S.V.P Received | Thank You Sent | Number Attending |
| --- | --- | --- | --- | --- |

Name

Address

Telephone Number

E-mail Address

Gift

| Save The Day Card Sent | Invitation Sent | R.S.V.P Received | Thank You Sent | Number Attending |
| --- | --- | --- | --- | --- |

Name

Address

Telephone Number

E-mail Address

Gift

| Save The Day Card Sent | Invitation Sent | R.S.V.P Received | Thank You Sent | Number Attending |
| --- | --- | --- | --- | --- |

Name

Address

Telephone Number

E-mail Address

Gift

| Save The Day Card Sent | Invitation Sent | R.S.V.P Received | Thank You Sent | Number Attending |
| --- | --- | --- | --- | --- |

# Guest List Planner

Name

Address

Telephone Number

E-mail Address

Gift

| Save The Day Card Sent | Invitation Sent | R.S.V.P Received | Thank You Sent | Number Attending |
|---|---|---|---|---|

Name

Address

Telephone Number

E-mail Address

Gift

| Save The Day Card Sent | Invitation Sent | R.S.V.P Received | Thank You Sent | Number Attending |
|---|---|---|---|---|

Name

Address

Telephone Number

E-mail Address

Gift

| Save The Day Card Sent | Invitation Sent | R.S.V.P Received | Thank You Sent | Number Attending |
|---|---|---|---|---|

Name

Address

Telephone Number

E-mail Address

Gift

| Save The Day Card Sent | Invitation Sent | R.S.V.P Received | Thank You Sent | Number Attending |
|---|---|---|---|---|

Name

Address

Telephone Number

E-mail Address

Gift

| Save The Day Card Sent | Invitation Sent | R.S.V.P Received | Thank You Sent | Number Attending |
|---|---|---|---|---|

# Guest List Planner

Name

Address

Telephone Number

E-mail Address

Gift

| Save The Day Card Sent | Invitation Sent | R.S.V.P Received | Thank You Sent | Number Attending |
| --- | --- | --- | --- | --- |

Name

Address

Telephone Number

E-mail Address

Gift

| Save The Day Card Sent | Invitation Sent | R.S.V.P Received | Thank You Sent | Number Attending |
| --- | --- | --- | --- | --- |

Name

Address

Telephone Number

E-mail Address

Gift

| Save The Day Card Sent | Invitation Sent | R.S.V.P Received | Thank You Sent | Number Attending |
| --- | --- | --- | --- | --- |

Name

Address

Telephone Number

E-mail Address

Gift

| Save The Day Card Sent | Invitation Sent | R.S.V.P Received | Thank You Sent | Number Attending |
| --- | --- | --- | --- | --- |

Name

Address

Telephone Number

E-mail Address

Gift

| Save The Day Card Sent | Invitation Sent | R.S.V.P Received | Thank You Sent | Number Attending |
| --- | --- | --- | --- | --- |

# Guest List Planner

Name

Address

Telephone Number

E-mail Address

Gift

| Save The Day<br>Card Sent | Invitation<br>Sent | R.S.V.P<br>Received | Thank You<br>Sent | Number<br>Attending |
| --- | --- | --- | --- | --- |

Name

Address

Telephone Number

E-mail Address

Gift

| Save The Day<br>Card Sent | Invitation<br>Sent | R.S.V.P<br>Received | Thank You<br>Sent | Number<br>Attending |
| --- | --- | --- | --- | --- |

Name

Address

Telephone Number

E-mail Address

Gift

| Save The Day<br>Card Sent | Invitation<br>Sent | R.S.V.P<br>Received | Thank You<br>Sent | Number<br>Attending |
| --- | --- | --- | --- | --- |

Name

Address

Telephone Number

E-mail Address

Gift

| Save The Day<br>Card Sent | Invitation<br>Sent | R.S.V.P<br>Received | Thank You<br>Sent | Number<br>Attending |
| --- | --- | --- | --- | --- |

Name

Address

Telephone Number

E-mail Address

Gift

| Save The Day<br>Card Sent | Invitation<br>Sent | R.S.V.P<br>Received | Thank You<br>Sent | Number<br>Attending |
| --- | --- | --- | --- | --- |

# Guest List Planner

Name
___________________________

Address
___________________________

Telephone Number
___________________________

E-mail Address
___________________________

Gift
___________________________

| Save The Day Card Sent | Invitation Sent | R.S.V.P Received | Thank You Sent | Number Attending |
| --- | --- | --- | --- | --- |
| | | | | |

Name
___________________________

Address
___________________________

Telephone Number
___________________________

E-mail Address
___________________________

Gift
___________________________

| Save The Day Card Sent | Invitation Sent | R.S.V.P Received | Thank You Sent | Number Attending |
| --- | --- | --- | --- | --- |
| | | | | |

Name
___________________________

Address
___________________________

Telephone Number
___________________________

E-mail Address
___________________________

Gift
___________________________

| Save The Day Card Sent | Invitation Sent | R.S.V.P Received | Thank You Sent | Number Attending |
| --- | --- | --- | --- | --- |
| | | | | |

Name
___________________________

Address
___________________________

Telephone Number
___________________________

E-mail Address
___________________________

Gift
___________________________

| Save The Day Card Sent | Invitation Sent | R.S.V.P Received | Thank You Sent | Number Attending |
| --- | --- | --- | --- | --- |
| | | | | |

Name
___________________________

Address
___________________________

Telephone Number
___________________________

E-mail Address
___________________________

Gift
___________________________

| Save The Day Card Sent | Invitation Sent | R.S.V.P Received | Thank You Sent | Number Attending |
| --- | --- | --- | --- | --- |
| | | | | |

# Guest List Planner

Name

Address

Telephone Number

E-mail Address

Gift

| Save The Day Card Sent | Invitation Sent | R.S.V.P Received | Thank You Sent | Number Attending |
| --- | --- | --- | --- | --- |
| | | | | |

Name

Address

Telephone Number

E-mail Address

Gift

| Save The Day Card Sent | Invitation Sent | R.S.V.P Received | Thank You Sent | Number Attending |
| --- | --- | --- | --- | --- |
| | | | | |

Name

Address

Telephone Number

E-mail Address

Gift

| Save The Day Card Sent | Invitation Sent | R.S.V.P Received | Thank You Sent | Number Attending |
| --- | --- | --- | --- | --- |
| | | | | |

Name

Address

Telephone Number

E-mail Address

Gift

| Save The Day Card Sent | Invitation Sent | R.S.V.P Received | Thank You Sent | Number Attending |
| --- | --- | --- | --- | --- |
| | | | | |

Name

Address

Telephone Number

E-mail Address

Gift

| Save The Day Card Sent | Invitation Sent | R.S.V.P Received | Thank You Sent | Number Attending |
| --- | --- | --- | --- | --- |
| | | | | |

# Guest List Planner

Name

Address

Telephone Number

E-mail Address

Gift

| Save The Day Card Sent | Invitation Sent | R.S.V.P Received | Thank You Sent | Number Attending |
| --- | --- | --- | --- | --- |

Name

Address

Telephone Number

E-mail Address

Gift

| Save The Day Card Sent | Invitation Sent | R.S.V.P Received | Thank You Sent | Number Attending |
| --- | --- | --- | --- | --- |

Name

Address

Telephone Number

E-mail Address

Gift

| Save The Day Card Sent | Invitation Sent | R.S.V.P Received | Thank You Sent | Number Attending |
| --- | --- | --- | --- | --- |

Name

Address

Telephone Number

E-mail Address

Gift

| Save The Day Card Sent | Invitation Sent | R.S.V.P Received | Thank You Sent | Number Attending |
| --- | --- | --- | --- | --- |

Name

Address

Telephone Number

E-mail Address

Gift

| Save The Day Card Sent | Invitation Sent | R.S.V.P Received | Thank You Sent | Number Attending |
| --- | --- | --- | --- | --- |

# Guest List Planner

Name
______________________________

Address
______________________________

Telephone Number
______________________________

E-mail Address
______________________________

Gift
______________________________

| Save The Day Card Sent | Invitation Sent | R.S.V.P Received | Thank You Sent | Number Attending |
|---|---|---|---|---|
| | | | | |

Name
______________________________

Address
______________________________

Telephone Number
______________________________

E-mail Address
______________________________

Gift
______________________________

| Save The Day Card Sent | Invitation Sent | R.S.V.P Received | Thank You Sent | Number Attending |
|---|---|---|---|---|
| | | | | |

Name
______________________________

Address
______________________________

Telephone Number
______________________________

E-mail Address
______________________________

Gift
______________________________

| Save The Day Card Sent | Invitation Sent | R.S.V.P Received | Thank You Sent | Number Attending |
|---|---|---|---|---|
| | | | | |

Name
______________________________

Address
______________________________

Telephone Number
______________________________

E-mail Address
______________________________

Gift
______________________________

| Save The Day Card Sent | Invitation Sent | R.S.V.P Received | Thank You Sent | Number Attending |
|---|---|---|---|---|
| | | | | |

Name
______________________________

Address
______________________________

Telephone Number
______________________________

E-mail Address
______________________________

Gift
______________________________

| Save The Day Card Sent | Invitation Sent | R.S.V.P Received | Thank You Sent | Number Attending |
|---|---|---|---|---|
| | | | | |

# *Guest List Planner*

Name

Address

Telephone Number

E-mail Address

Gift

| Save The Day Card Sent | Invitation Sent | R.S.V.P Received | Thank You Sent | Number Attending |
|---|---|---|---|---|

Name

Address

Telephone Number

E-mail Address

Gift

| Save The Day Card Sent | Invitation Sent | R.S.V.P Received | Thank You Sent | Number Attending |
|---|---|---|---|---|

Name

Address

Telephone Number

E-mail Address

Gift

| Save The Day Card Sent | Invitation Sent | R.S.V.P Received | Thank You Sent | Number Attending |
|---|---|---|---|---|

Name

Address

Telephone Number

E-mail Address

Gift

| Save The Day Card Sent | Invitation Sent | R.S.V.P Received | Thank You Sent | Number Attending |
|---|---|---|---|---|

Name

Address

Telephone Number

E-mail Address

Gift

| Save The Day Card Sent | Invitation Sent | R.S.V.P Received | Thank You Sent | Number Attending |
|---|---|---|---|---|

# Guest List Planner

Name

Address

Telephone Number

E-mail Address

Gift

| Save The Day Card Sent | Invitation Sent | R.S.V.P Received | Thank You Sent | Number Attending |
| --- | --- | --- | --- | --- |

Name

Address

Telephone Number

E-mail Address

Gift

| Save The Day Card Sent | Invitation Sent | R.S.V.P Received | Thank You Sent | Number Attending |
| --- | --- | --- | --- | --- |

Name

Address

Telephone Number

E-mail Address

Gift

| Save The Day Card Sent | Invitation Sent | R.S.V.P Received | Thank You Sent | Number Attending |
| --- | --- | --- | --- | --- |

Name

Address

Telephone Number

E-mail Address

Gift

| Save The Day Card Sent | Invitation Sent | R.S.V.P Received | Thank You Sent | Number Attending |
| --- | --- | --- | --- | --- |

Name

Address

Telephone Number

E-mail Address

Gift

| Save The Day Card Sent | Invitation Sent | R.S.V.P Received | Thank You Sent | Number Attending |
| --- | --- | --- | --- | --- |

# Guest List Planner

Name

Address

Telephone Number

E-mail Address

Gift

| Save The Day Card Sent | Invitation Sent | R.S.V.P Received | Thank You Sent | Number Attending |
|---|---|---|---|---|

Name

Address

Telephone Number

E-mail Address

Gift

| Save The Day Card Sent | Invitation Sent | R.S.V.P Received | Thank You Sent | Number Attending |
|---|---|---|---|---|

Name

Address

Telephone Number

E-mail Address

Gift

| Save The Day Card Sent | Invitation Sent | R.S.V.P Received | Thank You Sent | Number Attending |
|---|---|---|---|---|

Name

Address

Telephone Number

E-mail Address

Gift

| Save The Day Card Sent | Invitation Sent | R.S.V.P Received | Thank You Sent | Number Attending |
|---|---|---|---|---|

Name

Address

Telephone Number

E-mail Address

Gift

| Save The Day Card Sent | Invitation Sent | R.S.V.P Received | Thank You Sent | Number Attending |
|---|---|---|---|---|

# Guest List Planner

Name

Address

Telephone Number

E-mail Address

Gift

| Save The Day Card Sent | Invitation Sent | R.S.V.P Received | Thank You Sent | Number Attending |
|---|---|---|---|---|
|  |  |  |  |  |

Name

Address

Telephone Number

E-mail Address

Gift

| Save The Day Card Sent | Invitation Sent | R.S.V.P Received | Thank You Sent | Number Attending |
|---|---|---|---|---|
|  |  |  |  |  |

Name

Address

Telephone Number

E-mail Address

Gift

| Save The Day Card Sent | Invitation Sent | R.S.V.P Received | Thank You Sent | Number Attending |
|---|---|---|---|---|
|  |  |  |  |  |

Name

Address

Telephone Number

E-mail Address

Gift

| Save The Day Card Sent | Invitation Sent | R.S.V.P Received | Thank You Sent | Number Attending |
|---|---|---|---|---|
|  |  |  |  |  |

Name

Address

Telephone Number

E-mail Address

Gift

| Save The Day Card Sent | Invitation Sent | R.S.V.P Received | Thank You Sent | Number Attending |
|---|---|---|---|---|
|  |  |  |  |  |

# Guest List Planner

Name

Address

Telephone Number

E-mail Address

Gift

| Save The Day Card Sent | Invitation Sent | R.S.V.P Received | Thank You Sent | Number Attending |
| --- | --- | --- | --- | --- |

Name

Address

Telephone Number

E-mail Address

Gift

| Save The Day Card Sent | Invitation Sent | R.S.V.P Received | Thank You Sent | Number Attending |
| --- | --- | --- | --- | --- |

Name

Address

Telephone Number

E-mail Address

Gift

| Save The Day Card Sent | Invitation Sent | R.S.V.P Received | Thank You Sent | Number Attending |
| --- | --- | --- | --- | --- |

Name

Address

Telephone Number

E-mail Address

Gift

| Save The Day Card Sent | Invitation Sent | R.S.V.P Received | Thank You Sent | Number Attending |
| --- | --- | --- | --- | --- |

Name

Address

Telephone Number

E-mail Address

Gift

| Save The Day Card Sent | Invitation Sent | R.S.V.P Received | Thank You Sent | Number Attending |
| --- | --- | --- | --- | --- |

# Guest List Planner

Name

Address

Telephone Number

E-mail Address

Gift

| Save The Day Card Sent | Invitation Sent | R.S.V.P Received | Thank You Sent | Number Attending |
|---|---|---|---|---|

Name

Address

Telephone Number

E-mail Address

Gift

| Save The Day Card Sent | Invitation Sent | R.S.V.P Received | Thank You Sent | Number Attending |
|---|---|---|---|---|

Name

Address

Telephone Number

E-mail Address

Gift

| Save The Day Card Sent | Invitation Sent | R.S.V.P Received | Thank You Sent | Number Attending |
|---|---|---|---|---|

Name

Address

Telephone Number

E-mail Address

Gift

| Save The Day Card Sent | Invitation Sent | R.S.V.P Received | Thank You Sent | Number Attending |
|---|---|---|---|---|

Name

Address

Telephone Number

E-mail Address

Gift

| Save The Day Card Sent | Invitation Sent | R.S.V.P Received | Thank You Sent | Number Attending |
|---|---|---|---|---|

# Guest List Planner

Name

Address

Telephone Number

E-mail Address

Gift

| Save The Day Card Sent | Invitation Sent | R.S.V.P Received | Thank You Sent | Number Attending |
| --- | --- | --- | --- | --- |

Name

Address

Telephone Number

E-mail Address

Gift

| Save The Day Card Sent | Invitation Sent | R.S.V.P Received | Thank You Sent | Number Attending |
| --- | --- | --- | --- | --- |

Name

Address

Telephone Number

E-mail Address

Gift

| Save The Day Card Sent | Invitation Sent | R.S.V.P Received | Thank You Sent | Number Attending |
| --- | --- | --- | --- | --- |

Name

Address

Telephone Number

E-mail Address

Gift

| Save The Day Card Sent | Invitation Sent | R.S.V.P Received | Thank You Sent | Number Attending |
| --- | --- | --- | --- | --- |

Name

Address

Telephone Number

E-mail Address

Gift

| Save The Day Card Sent | Invitation Sent | R.S.V.P Received | Thank You Sent | Number Attending |
| --- | --- | --- | --- | --- |

# Guest List Planner

Name
_______________________________________________

Address
_______________________________________________

Telephone Number
_______________________________________________

E-mail Address
_______________________________________________

Gift
_______________________________________________

| Save The Day Card Sent | Invitation Sent | R.S.V.P Received | Thank You Sent | Number Attending |
| --- | --- | --- | --- | --- |
| | | | | |

Name
_______________________________________________

Address
_______________________________________________

Telephone Number
_______________________________________________

E-mail Address
_______________________________________________

Gift
_______________________________________________

| Save The Day Card Sent | Invitation Sent | R.S.V.P Received | Thank You Sent | Number Attending |
| --- | --- | --- | --- | --- |
| | | | | |

Name
_______________________________________________

Address
_______________________________________________

Telephone Number
_______________________________________________

E-mail Address
_______________________________________________

Gift
_______________________________________________

| Save The Day Card Sent | Invitation Sent | R.S.V.P Received | Thank You Sent | Number Attending |
| --- | --- | --- | --- | --- |
| | | | | |

Name
_______________________________________________

Address
_______________________________________________

Telephone Number
_______________________________________________

E-mail Address
_______________________________________________

Gift
_______________________________________________

| Save The Day Card Sent | Invitation Sent | R.S.V.P Received | Thank You Sent | Number Attending |
| --- | --- | --- | --- | --- |
| | | | | |

Name
_______________________________________________

Address
_______________________________________________

Telephone Number
_______________________________________________

E-mail Address
_______________________________________________

Gift
_______________________________________________

| Save The Day Card Sent | Invitation Sent | R.S.V.P Received | Thank You Sent | Number Attending |
| --- | --- | --- | --- | --- |
| | | | | |

# Guest List Planner

Name

Address

Telephone Number

E-mail Address

Gift

| Save The Day Card Sent | Invitation Sent | R.S.V.P Received | Thank You Sent | Number Attending |
| --- | --- | --- | --- | --- |

Name

Address

Telephone Number

E-mail Address

Gift

| Save The Day Card Sent | Invitation Sent | R.S.V.P Received | Thank You Sent | Number Attending |
| --- | --- | --- | --- | --- |

Name

Address

Telephone Number

E-mail Address

Gift

| Save The Day Card Sent | Invitation Sent | R.S.V.P Received | Thank You Sent | Number Attending |
| --- | --- | --- | --- | --- |

Name

Address

Telephone Number

E-mail Address

Gift

| Save The Day Card Sent | Invitation Sent | R.S.V.P Received | Thank You Sent | Number Attending |
| --- | --- | --- | --- | --- |

Name

Address

Telephone Number

E-mail Address

Gift

| Save The Day Card Sent | Invitation Sent | R.S.V.P Received | Thank You Sent | Number Attending |
| --- | --- | --- | --- | --- |

# Guest List Planner

Name

Address

Telephone Number

E-mail Address

Gift

| Save The Day Card Sent | Invitation Sent | R.S.V.P Received | Thank You Sent | Number Attending |
| --- | --- | --- | --- | --- |
|  |  |  |  |  |

Name

Address

Telephone Number

E-mail Address

Gift

| Save The Day Card Sent | Invitation Sent | R.S.V.P Received | Thank You Sent | Number Attending |
| --- | --- | --- | --- | --- |
|  |  |  |  |  |

Name

Address

Telephone Number

E-mail Address

Gift

| Save The Day Card Sent | Invitation Sent | R.S.V.P Received | Thank You Sent | Number Attending |
| --- | --- | --- | --- | --- |
|  |  |  |  |  |

Name

Address

Telephone Number

E-mail Address

Gift

| Save The Day Card Sent | Invitation Sent | R.S.V.P Received | Thank You Sent | Number Attending |
| --- | --- | --- | --- | --- |
|  |  |  |  |  |

Name

Address

Telephone Number

E-mail Address

Gift

| Save The Day Card Sent | Invitation Sent | R.S.V.P Received | Thank You Sent | Number Attending |
| --- | --- | --- | --- | --- |
|  |  |  |  |  |

# Guest List Planner

Name

Address

Telephone Number

E-mail Address

Gift

| Save The Day Card Sent | Invitation Sent | R.S.V.P Received | Thank You Sent | Number Attending |
| --- | --- | --- | --- | --- |

Name

Address

Telephone Number

E-mail Address

Gift

| Save The Day Card Sent | Invitation Sent | R.S.V.P Received | Thank You Sent | Number Attending |
| --- | --- | --- | --- | --- |

Name

Address

Telephone Number

E-mail Address

Gift

| Save The Day Card Sent | Invitation Sent | R.S.V.P Received | Thank You Sent | Number Attending |
| --- | --- | --- | --- | --- |

Name

Address

Telephone Number

E-mail Address

Gift

| Save The Day Card Sent | Invitation Sent | R.S.V.P Received | Thank You Sent | Number Attending |
| --- | --- | --- | --- | --- |

Name

Address

Telephone Number

E-mail Address

Gift

| Save The Day Card Sent | Invitation Sent | R.S.V.P Received | Thank You Sent | Number Attending |
| --- | --- | --- | --- | --- |

# Guest List Planner

Name

Address

Telephone Number

E-mail Address

Gift

| Save The Day Card Sent | Invitation Sent | R.S.V.P Received | Thank You Sent | Number Attending |
| --- | --- | --- | --- | --- |

Name

Address

Telephone Number

E-mail Address

Gift

| Save The Day Card Sent | Invitation Sent | R.S.V.P Received | Thank You Sent | Number Attending |
| --- | --- | --- | --- | --- |

Name

Address

Telephone Number

E-mail Address

Gift

| Save The Day Card Sent | Invitation Sent | R.S.V.P Received | Thank You Sent | Number Attending |
| --- | --- | --- | --- | --- |

Name

Address

Telephone Number

E-mail Address

Gift

| Save The Day Card Sent | Invitation Sent | R.S.V.P Received | Thank You Sent | Number Attending |
| --- | --- | --- | --- | --- |

Name

Address

Telephone Number

E-mail Address

Gift

| Save The Day Card Sent | Invitation Sent | R.S.V.P Received | Thank You Sent | Number Attending |
| --- | --- | --- | --- | --- |

# Guest List Planner

Name

Address

Telephone Number

E-mail Address

Gift

| Save The Day Card Sent | Invitation Sent | R.S.V.P Received | Thank You Sent | Number Attending |
|---|---|---|---|---|

Name

Address

Telephone Number

E-mail Address

Gift

| Save The Day Card Sent | Invitation Sent | R.S.V.P Received | Thank You Sent | Number Attending |
|---|---|---|---|---|

Name

Address

Telephone Number

E-mail Address

Gift

| Save The Day Card Sent | Invitation Sent | R.S.V.P Received | Thank You Sent | Number Attending |
|---|---|---|---|---|

Name

Address

Telephone Number

E-mail Address

Gift

| Save The Day Card Sent | Invitation Sent | R.S.V.P Received | Thank You Sent | Number Attending |
|---|---|---|---|---|

Name

Address

Telephone Number

E-mail Address

Gift

| Save The Day Card Sent | Invitation Sent | R.S.V.P Received | Thank You Sent | Number Attending |
|---|---|---|---|---|

# Guest List Planner

Name

Address

Telephone Number

E-mail Address

Gift

| Save The Day Card Sent | Invitation Sent | R.S.V.P Received | Thank You Sent | Number Attending |
| --- | --- | --- | --- | --- |

Name

Address

Telephone Number

E-mail Address

Gift

| Save The Day Card Sent | Invitation Sent | R.S.V.P Received | Thank You Sent | Number Attending |
| --- | --- | --- | --- | --- |

Name

Address

Telephone Number

E-mail Address

Gift

| Save The Day Card Sent | Invitation Sent | R.S.V.P Received | Thank You Sent | Number Attending |
| --- | --- | --- | --- | --- |

Name

Address

Telephone Number

E-mail Address

Gift

| Save The Day Card Sent | Invitation Sent | R.S.V.P Received | Thank You Sent | Number Attending |
| --- | --- | --- | --- | --- |

Name

Address

Telephone Number

E-mail Address

Gift

| Save The Day Card Sent | Invitation Sent | R.S.V.P Received | Thank You Sent | Number Attending |
| --- | --- | --- | --- | --- |

# Guest List Planner

Name

Address

Telephone Number

E-mail Address

Gift

| Save The Day Card Sent | Invitation Sent | R.S.V.P Received | Thank You Sent | Number Attending |
| --- | --- | --- | --- | --- |
|  |  |  |  |  |

Name

Address

Telephone Number

E-mail Address

Gift

| Save The Day Card Sent | Invitation Sent | R.S.V.P Received | Thank You Sent | Number Attending |
| --- | --- | --- | --- | --- |
|  |  |  |  |  |

Name

Address

Telephone Number

E-mail Address

Gift

| Save The Day Card Sent | Invitation Sent | R.S.V.P Received | Thank You Sent | Number Attending |
| --- | --- | --- | --- | --- |
|  |  |  |  |  |

Name

Address

Telephone Number

E-mail Address

Gift

| Save The Day Card Sent | Invitation Sent | R.S.V.P Received | Thank You Sent | Number Attending |
| --- | --- | --- | --- | --- |
|  |  |  |  |  |

Name

Address

Telephone Number

E-mail Address

Gift

| Save The Day Card Sent | Invitation Sent | R.S.V.P Received | Thank You Sent | Number Attending |
| --- | --- | --- | --- | --- |
|  |  |  |  |  |

# Guest List Planner

Name

Address

Telephone Number

E-mail Address

Gift

| Save The Day Card Sent | Invitation Sent | R.S.V.P Received | Thank You Sent | Number Attending |
| --- | --- | --- | --- | --- |

Name

Address

Telephone Number

E-mail Address

Gift

| Save The Day Card Sent | Invitation Sent | R.S.V.P Received | Thank You Sent | Number Attending |
| --- | --- | --- | --- | --- |

Name

Address

Telephone Number

E-mail Address

Gift

| Save The Day Card Sent | Invitation Sent | R.S.V.P Received | Thank You Sent | Number Attending |
| --- | --- | --- | --- | --- |

Name

Address

Telephone Number

E-mail Address

Gift

| Save The Day Card Sent | Invitation Sent | R.S.V.P Received | Thank You Sent | Number Attending |
| --- | --- | --- | --- | --- |

Name

Address

Telephone Number

E-mail Address

Gift

| Save The Day Card Sent | Invitation Sent | R.S.V.P Received | Thank You Sent | Number Attending |
| --- | --- | --- | --- | --- |